MODERN AFRICAN SPIRITUALITY

MODERN AFRICAN SPIRITUALITY
The Independent Holy Spirit Churches
in East Africa, 1902–1976

ANE MARIE BAK RASMUSSEN

British Academic Press
London · New York

Published in 1996 by
British Academic Press
An imprint of I.B. Tauris & Co Ltd
45 Bloomsbury Square
London WC1A 2HY

175 Fifth Avenue
New York
NY 10010

In the United States of America
and Canada distributed by
St Martin's Press
175 Fifth Avenue
New York
NY 10010

A full CIP record for this book is available from the British Library

Library of Congress catalog card number: 95–61526
A full CIP record is available from the Library of Congress

ISBN 1–86064–001–X

Copy-edited and laser-set by Selro Publishing Services, Oxford
Printed and bound in Great Britain by WBC Ltd, Bridgend, Mid
Glamorgan

Contents

Maps and Illustrations

Maps

Illustrations

Glossary

avahuji	people who have broken away, separatists
avakambuli	those who say what they have to (confess) openly
Avandu va Roho	People of the Spirit
dini	religion
Dini ya Roho	Religion of the Spirit
Evangeli ya Roho Mtakatifu	Gospel Holy Spirit (Luragoli)
evimbi (wele)	evil god (Lubukusu)
Gi twulidzwe!	may it be taken away!
gumali (wele)	black god (Lubukusu)
Hodi?	May I come in?
Joroho	People of the Spirit (Dholuo)
khwitakasa	to clean, wash (cleanse their hearts)
kipande	registration card
lilinda	waiting
livukana	meeting, church service
Lyahuka	a group that has broken away
mademoni	demons
misambwa	ancestors
mtakatifu	holy
omukumu	diviner
omung'oli	dream-prophet
omuwanga	white
sadaka	collection
Watu wa Roho	People of the Spirit (Kiswahili)
wele	god
Yesu akhusamehe	May Jesus forgive you
Yesu yasamehe	Jesus, forgive me

Preface and Acknowledgements

The contents of this book were once part of a larger manuscript, 'Contextualization of the Church in Kenya, Illustrated through the Society of Friends and the Holy Spirit Churches in Western Kenya', which Ane Marie Bak Rasmussen had planned to complete by the end of 1993. At the time of her death on 19 October 1992 only the first part, on the Society of Friends, had been fully completed. Ane Marie had already done fieldwork for the second part, on the Holy Spirit Churches, and parts of her Master of Arts thesis. She had planned to integrate her thesis, originally entitled 'The History and Present Characteristics of Four African Independent Churches in Western Kenya: Holy Spirit Church of East Africa, African Church of the Holy Spirit, Gospel Holy Spirit Church of East Africa and Lyahuka Church of East Africa' (1976), into the second part of the manuscript. Because of technical difficulties, the thesis was withdrawn from Nairobi University without examination. *Modern African Spirituality: The Independent Holy Spirit Churches in East Africa, 1902–1976* by the late Ane Marie Bak Rasmussen should therefore be regarded as a sequel to her first book, *A History of the Quaker Movement in Africa*, which was published by British Academic Press in January 1995.

Ane Marie Bak Rasmussen began her fieldwork in western Kenya in 1974. She was fascinated by the Holy Spirit Churches, the African independent Churches that had broken away from the Friends Church. She was especially fascinated by the members' experiences of being filled with the Holy Spirit — a closeness to God through which evil was overcome. Ane Marie first spent two years (from 1974 to 1976) in Kenya; thereafter, until 1991, she did research there for longer and shorter periods in order to follow developments within the Friends and Holy Spirit churches, and to observe the contrasts and similarities between them.

To find out how Friends think and live — in the USA, from where most of the missionaries came, as well as in Britain where it all started in the seventeenth century — and to learn about the historical development of the Friends movement, in 1985 Ane Marie visited the Wider Ministries Commission (under the Friends United Meeting in Richmond, Indiana) and the Friends' Study Centre at Woodbrooke College, Selly Oak, Birmingham, England. These are Ane Marie's own acknowledgements, written shortly before her death:

My interest in western Kenya was first sparked off by discussions with my husband, Joseph Wasike Mululu. He and I have done all the field research together since 1974, and without his intimate knowledge of the area and its people I would not have been able to have made so many valuable contacts or to have reached the same level of understanding. Whenever we visited churches in Kenya, whether Quaker or Holy Spirit, we were always made to feel we were coming back to good friends. This made it possible to share intimate feelings and knowledge about what was going on. Despite all the splits that have occurred and which in some cases have made it difficult for people from different groups to meet and talk together in a constructive way, we have been received everywhere as friends and have been given the information that was necessary to allow us to form a balanced view of the situation. I thank my husband for his tireless work and all our good friends in Kenya, Quakers as well as members of the Holy Spirit churches, for the trust they put in us. And I hope that what I have written in this book may reflect and respect their trust. I should like to mention specifically a few of the persons with whom I have talked several times over the years. These include G. Jeremiah Lusweti, Thomas Ganira Lung'aho, Elisha Wakube, Ezekiel Wanyonyi, George Kamwesa, Solomon Adagala and Timotheo Hezekiah Shitsimi, as well as the late Kefa Ayub Mavuru, Japhet Zale Ambula and Eliakim Keverenge Atonya. The names of many others are to be found in the book, but I have talked with so many people that it has been impossible to mention them all.

Outside Kenya, I would like to thank the staff of the

Friends United Meeting in Richmond, Indiana, USA, for giving me access to their records where I learnt much about the missionaries who went to Kenya and, through their writings, about the history of the Friends churches in Kenya. I also thank the librarians at Earlham College (also in Richmond, Indiana) for allowing me to use their library and its facilities. A number of Friends in Richmond helped me in many practical ways and tried to give me an understanding of the historical and contemporary life of Quakers. I give special thanks to Louise and Jay Beede, who received me as a guest in their house for the entire period of about six weeks I spent in Richmond, and to Evelyn and Harold V. Smuck, who arranged everything for me before my arrival.

Likewise, I learnt a considerable amount about the origins and development of Quakerism during my stay in England at Woodbrooke College, Selly Oak, Birmingham in late 1985. I thank the staff of Woodbrooke College for all the help they gave me.

Finally, I wish to thank Professor Johannes Aagaard, my supervisor at the University of Aarhus through these many years of study, for his readiness to give advice and help at all times. I also very much appreciate the help of Professors Anna Marie Aagaard, Lars Thunberg and Holger Bernt Hansen, who read my manuscript and gave me much valuable advice.

In addition to these acknowledgements, expressed by Ane Marie herself, I want to mention some further names of people and organizations who deserve our appreciation. This book could not have been completed without the goodwill and assistance of the Kenyan government and the four independent Holy Spirit Churches in western Kenya. I am grateful to all the members, leaders and founders of Holy Spirit Churches who kept us thinking and learning as well as talking about Christian values. I am grateful to them for showing us the importance of the Holy Spirit, for being people, for the time we spent simply being present, for their hospitality and for their help in our immediate personal problem over a long-term plan. Their church is a family, an extended household.

I owe thanks to officials in the Office of the President and in the

Provincial Administration and Internal Security in Nairobi, who issued the research permit and made it possible to collect relevant information, and to the authorities of the Provincial Administration for Western Province, in Kakamega and in Bungoma District. I owe thanks to members of the Friends Church in Kenya, to students and staff at the Friends Theological College (formerly Friends Bible Institute) in Tiriki, at the St Paul's United Theological College in Limuru and at Friends centres in Kolokol, Turkana and Lodwar in Kenya, as well as at the Makumira Theological College at Usa River in Arusha, Tanzania.

Further thanks are due to the staff of the Kenya National Archives and Documentation Service in Nairobi; to the National Council of Churches of Kenya in Nairobi; to the All Africa Conference of Churches in Nairobi; to John Padwick of the Organization of African Instituted Churches in Nairobi; to the head of the Roman Catholic Church in Nairobi, His Eminence Maurice M. Cardinal Otunga; to the sisters of Tindinyo Carmel in Kaimosi; to the headmistress of the Mukumu Girls' High School, Sister Rita Itebete; and to the late Father Agapitus Muse of the Mukumu Roman Catholic Mission.

I would like to thank Thomas and Leah Ganira of the Madioli Friends Church in Shinyalu, Isukha; Josiah Embego of the Chambiti Friends Church in Maragoli; G. Jeremiah and Rachel Lusweti of the Butunde Friends Church in Chwele, Bungoma; J. K. Mulira of Kakamega, the former provincial director of education for Western Province; S. E. Bunyali; E. P. Nakitare, the former director of culture in Nairobi; Faris and Dr J. A. Bukhala; Joseph Muliro, the former ambassador of Kenya to Sweden and other Nordic countries, and his wife, Lena.

I also wish to express my gratitude to Professor J. G. Dongers, Dr S. G. Kibicho and Dr E. M. Kasiera of the Department of Philosophy and Religious Studies; Dr Atieno-Odhiambo and Dr V. G. Simiyu of the History Department; Professor Simiyu Wandibba, director of the Institute of African Studies at the University of Nairobi; Professor Daniel N. Sifuna of the Education Foundation; Dr O. E. J. Shiroya of the History Department; Dr (Sister) Anne Nasimiyu, of the Philosophy and Religious Studies Department at Kenyatta University in Nairobi; Dr Chris W. Mukwa of the Faculty of Education; Julius and Susan Wasike of Moi University in Eldoret; Professor E. A. Anandele of the

University of Calabar in Nigeria; Dr Harold W. Turner, secretary of the Gospel and Cultures Trust in Remeura, Auckland, New Zealand; Evelyn and Professor J. W. Mukhwana of the Faculty of Business at Victoria University of Technology in Melbourne, Australia; Heiderrali Bhanji Noormohamed of North Vancouver BC, Canada; Martin, Lene, Eunice M. and Zadock McWere, Barbara D. and Ebbe Münster, and Marianne Üspeert of Amsterdam in The Netherlands.

Further thanks go to Inga and Sven Rasmussen; Jevenal, Rose, Fulton and Arnold Shiundu; Zeph and Monica Wekesa; Amos and Agnes Muricho of London; Beth Tomkinson of Oxford, UK; former Senior Chief Jonathan Barasa and his wife Ruth; Marianne Buer of Munich, Germany; Ben S. Wegesa; T. W. Wamunyokoli; John Kitui; E. M. Waliaula; George Wabuke; Nathan Munoko; Hezekiah Ngoya, Lynne Mansure; Marte Kari; Aage and Kristian Berntzen; Rolf and Miriam Bergh, Arthur and Alice Berntzen; Øyvind and Aud Bergh; Føbe and Edvin Frislie (Norwegian Pentecostal Church); Haldis and Hans Skuterud; Harald and Karin Bjørke; Ingjald Bolstad, Voss FHS, Terje Thronaes, and Elverum FHS of Norway; Ebba and Gösta Vestlund, and Nack, Ingrid and Johan Norbeck of Linköping in Sweden; M. W. Furaha; Hans, Vita and Mette Bak Rasmussen; Rigmor and Preben Frederiksen; Lone Bak Andersen and the late Kirsten Jensen; Hedvig and Alfred Bak Rasmussen; Karen and Axel Christensen; and Martin Pedersen.

My thanks too to Cie, Lene and Hans Pedersen; Ruth and Niels Jensen; Ane Mette Jensen; Jens and Anne Vibeke Mou; Karen Margrethe Honoré; Reuben, Margit and Louise Nsofor; Ellen Torben and Else Maria Thomsen; Lene and Maria Nielsen of Kama; Hans Aage and Christian Mink; Veronica M. Møller; Annette and the late Eugene Okoye; Revd Annemarie Bach Espensen; Zakaria and Roda Kwanusu Mululu; Wilber M. Wekesa; Ezekiel W. Kw M; Peter M. and Jane M. Wasike; K. Lynne; M. Wycliffe; S. M. Tesfai; Tekebash, Isayes, Awate and Yonnas Debessai; Reijo Kauppila; Etela-Pohjanmman Opisto; and Ilmajoki Heikki Sederlöf of the Finnish Folk High School Association in Helsinki, Finland. Also to Revd Kaj Ross-Hansen; Skrydstrup Præsteembede, Vojens; Revd Niels Jacobsen of Bjergby, Hjørring, Denmark, ambassador of the Republic of Kenya to Sweden and other Nordic countries; and Professor A. I.

Salim and his wife Monira Salim, for their helpful sense of perspective.

I wish to express sincere appreciation to Professor Anna Maria Aagaard, of the University of Aarhus Department of Systematic Theology's Section for Dogmatics; Professor Holger Bernt Hansen, director of the Centre of African Studies at the University of Copenhagen; Dr Jens Holger Schjorring, lecturer in the Department of Systematic Theology, Faculty of Theology, University of Aarhus; Bente Staer, the secretary in the Department of Systematic Theology at the University of Aarhus; Professor Kirsten Nielsen of the Department of Biblical Studies' Section for Old Testament Studies at the University of Aarhus; Professor Johannes Aagaard of the Department of Systematic Theology's Section for Missiology and Ecumenical Theology at the University of Aarhus; Professor Kathleen A. Staudt of the Department of Political Science at the University of Texas in El Paso, USA; Evelyn and the late Harold V. Smuck; Louise and Jay Beed of the Friends United Meeting in Richmond, Indiana, USA; and finally Dr Lester Crook of British Academic Press, London, who gave editorial advice and was responsible for the final editing and processing of the manuscript for publication. They all committed themselves to bringing about the speedy publication of Ane Marie's work and for this I wish to thank them.

Appreciation also goes to the various institutions that funded both Ane Marie's research at different periods and the publication of this book. These are the Lutheran World Federation in Geneva, Switzerland; the Scandinavian Institute of African Studies in Uppsala, Sweden; the Department of Systematic Theology at the University of Aarhus; the Danish Research Council for the Humanities; and Jens Norregaards og Hal Kochs Mindefond of Copenhagen; Aarhus Universitets Forskningsfond and Carlsbergfondet, Copenhagen.

Finally, a word of sincere thanks goes to our two sons, Hans Peter Bak Wasike Mululu and Zakarias Bak Wasike Mululu for their forbearance during the period of research in Kenya, the USA and the UK.

They have known many days when we were absent from home and play, and many evenings when we worked late. Also, they quietly gave the right kind of support and help at the appropriate times. I hope one day they will find inspiration in the work to which their mother was applied herself. We continue to look back and cherish the years of companionship, friendship, love and affection within our family.

Joseph Wasike Mululu
Aarhus, October 1995

Foreword

In her book on the history of the Quaker Church in western Kenya, Ane Marie Bak Rasmussen presented a thorough analysis of the Friends' missionary enterprise starting with the extraordinary growth in the number of Christians, the establishment of a Church under African leadership in the postwar years and finally the division of the Society of Friends into Four Yearly Meetings.

Interwoven with this development is the start of a spirit movement within the Friends Africa Mission in the late 1920s and gradually the establishment of four independent Churches, called Holy Spirit Churches. These are the topic of the present volume which represents a careful analysis of this most remarkable feature of African Christianity, the independent Churches. Not least, Kenya is interesting in this respect as it represents one of the most important areas for this special African phenomenon.

When we look back on Ane Marie Bak Rasmussen's many years of intensive research work into what she herself called 'Contextualization of the Church in Kenya', we can amidst all sadness congratulate ourselves that she managed to accomplish so much that it is possible both to present the results from the two main streams of her research and to make some comparative assessments between the two.

One common feature is the prevalence of African leadership. It is remarkable that compared to other missionary societies in East Africa the American Quaker Mission in Kenya tried at a very early stage to solve the classic problem of the relationship between mission and church by handing the authority and governing power to Africans. African requests for leadership and independence were met even before they appeared in the political arena. Hence it is ironic that at a time when the political independence had arrived the East Africa Yearly Meeting of Friends split into four separate churches (i.e. Yearly Meetings). Which factors can explain such a course of events?

Similarly, since the 1920s the Quaker Society had experienced a split by the secession of a group of Christians who were influenced by a spiritual revival and eventually formed the Holy Spirit movement. Again it is ironic that starting in 1950 the Holy Spirit movement experienced a number of secessions resulting in the four independent Churches which are the main objects of analysis in the present volume. Again, which factors can explain this turn of events?

In the opinion of Ane Marie Bak Rasmussen the explanation is close at hand and the same in both cases. The overriding factor is the conditions in the traditional society. Divisions between or within the ethnic groups supported by economic differentiation and in some cases personal rivalry account for the emergence of the different Churches. It follows as an important observation that the unitary ideology which Christianity represents cannot bridge the cleavages originating from the traditional society. This is an observation that has a general value for the whole East African setting — and even beyond. When a unitary ideology like Christianity is weighed against traditional structures the latter seem to prevail. Even when it comes to a kind of Christian pluralism by the emergence of several Churches, divisions in the traditional society take priority. The religious structures, especially the Church organizations, cannot be credited with a capability to neutralize or weaken the horizontal divisions supported by structures in the traditional society. The experience from this and other cases in East Africa is that the ethnic factor has shown itself to be superior to the religious factor.

Another important explanatory factor is the difference in attitude to the secular authority, be it the colonial or the independent government. Especially the independent Churches were looked upon with suspicion by the government in power as they were mirroring the ethnic and social divisions among the Luyia in western Kenya. By their strengthening of the traditional divisions and their acting as spokesmen for the local societies they could easily assume a political role. The mixing of religion and politics was close at hand and clearly a risk.

Hence the Kenyan government both before and after independence introduced various sets of rules aiming at guiding and controlling the behaviour of religious societies like the ones in western Kenya. Some of the Churches complied with the rules in order to improve their conditions of work while others took a more hostile attitude against interference.

Ane Marie Bak Rasmussen has taken a special interest in this major topic of church–state relations, not least manifested in a paper she gave to a conference on 'Religion and Politics in East Africa' held in Denmark in September 1990. This represents one of her latest pieces of work, and it was clearly influenced by the increase in ethnic tensions which were noticeable in her area of interest. However, she could not foresee how topical this whole development has turned out to be in view of later tragic events in western Kenya.

This makes her analysis of the relationship between the Churches and Daniel Arap Moi's government in the 1980s the more interesting. Following the president's growing concern it seemed only natural that in a number of cases local government officials intervened in the conflicts among Quakers 'in the interests of peace and security in the Church and the Country'. On the other hand the political role of the various churches seems to be caused by events in the non-religious environment. In other words, a political role cannot be ruled out, but it is primarily an 'ascribed' one and not a deliberately 'assumed' one.

The strongest message from Ane Marie Bak Rasmussen's analysis is that the Holy Spirit Churches provide 'a place to feel at home', a new identity and fellowship for people during a period of change. They care for both the material and the spiritual aspects of people's life, and they emphasize the unity of the sacred and the secular which used to be such a characteristic feature of traditional society.

It means that the Holy Spirit Churches are not alienating their followers from the traditional society, on the contrary they are supporting their feeling of belonging. In that respect they tend to value the local, small-scale societies and not the nation-wide elements of the mission Churches. And even more important, they incorporate elements of the traditional religion into Christianity, thus bridging the gap between the traditional value system and the Christian values.

This latter point emphasizes that the theology of the Holy Spirit Churches is crucial for an understanding of the whole course of events. Ane Marie Bak Rasmussen's book goes to the heart of probably the most genuine development on the African continent by its discussion of the current process of acculturation: the merging of Christianity and African traditional religion.

Holger Bernt Hansen
Professor of Church History and African Studies
University of Copenhagen

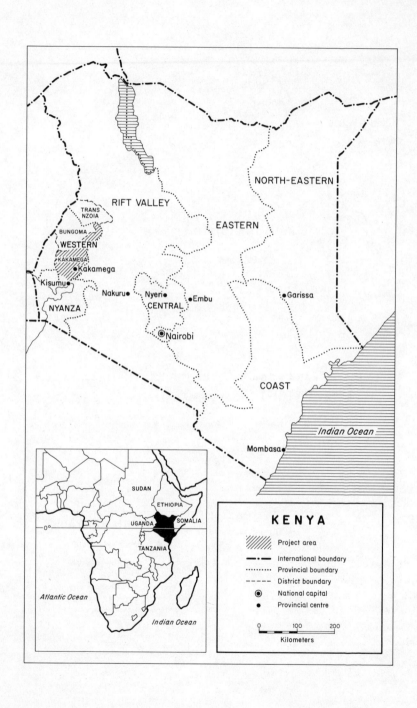

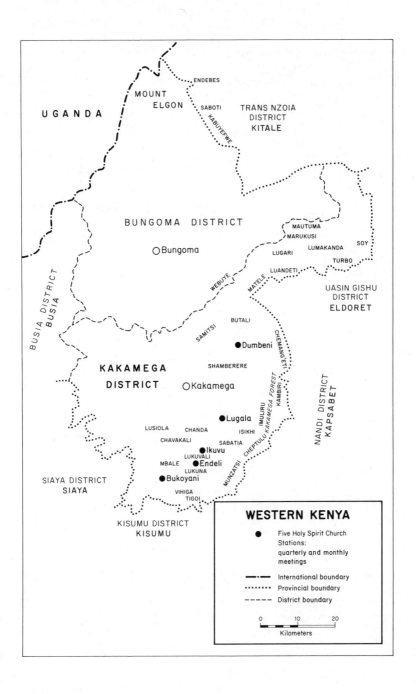

WESTERN KENYA

●   Five Holy Spirit Church Stations: quarterly and monthly meetings

—·—·—   International boundary

· · · · · · ·   Provincial boundary

– – – –   District boundary

0   10   20

Kilometers

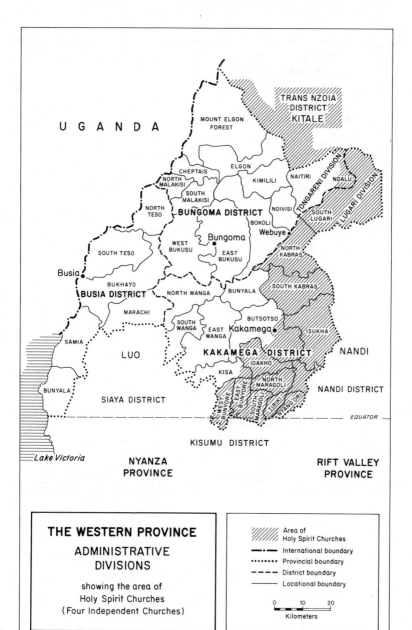

UGANDA

TRANS NZOIA
DISTRICT
KITALE

MOUNT ELGON
FOREST

ELGON

CHEPTAIS

NORTH
MALAKISI

SOUTH
MALAKISI

NORTH
TESO

KIMILILI

NAITIRI

NDALU

BUNGOMA DISTRICT

NDIVISI

TONGARENI DIVISION

LUGARI DIVISION

SOUTH
LUGARI

BOKOLI

Webuye

Bungoma

WEST
BUKUSU

EAST
BUKUSU

NORTH
KABRAS

SOUTH TESO

Busia

BUKHAYO

BUSIA DISTRICT

NORTH WANGA

BUNYALA

SOUTH KABRAS

MARACHI

SOUTH
WANGA

EAST
WANGA

BUTSOTSO

Kakamega

ISUKHA

NANDI

SAMIA

LUO

KAKAMEGA DISTRICT

KISA

IDAKHO

NANDI DISTRICT

BUNYALA

SIAYA DISTRICT

WEST
BUNYORE

EAST
BUNYORE

NORTH
MARAGOLI

SOUTH
MARAGOLI

TIRIKI

NYANG'ORI

EQUATOR

KISUMU DISTRICT

Lake Victoria

NYANZA
PROVINCE

RIFT VALLEY
PROVINCE

THE WESTERN PROVINCE

ADMINISTRATIVE
DIVISIONS

showing the area of
Holy Spirit Churches
(Four Independent Churches)

Area of
Holy Spirit Churches

International boundary

Provincial boundary

District boundary

Locational boundary

0   10   20

Kilometers

Introduction

African independent Churches form an important part of the total ecclesiastical set-up in Africa south of the Sahara. They have a long history in that the first separatist group to split from a mission Church did this in Sierra Leone as early as 1819 (Barrett 1968: 18). Today there are about 5000 independent Churches in 34 African nations, with members drawn from 290 tribes and a total membership of nearly seven million (Barrett 1968: 3).[1] Southern Africa has the greatest number of independent Churches, with the Republic of South Africa, where as much as a quarter of the African population are members of one or another of the independent Churches, having more adherents than any other country on the continent (Barrett 1968: 2). Compared with the rest of Africa, the number of independent Churches in East Africa is not very high. While the East African countries differ in this respect and while there are not very many of these Churches in Uganda and Tanzania, there are large numbers of them in Kenya where their membership is about 1.8 million (Barrett et al. 1973: 160). Here again, there are parts of the country without any independent Churches at all, while in other parts the density is very high. The highest number is found in Western and Nyanza Provinces in the western part of the country (Barrett 1968: 50).

Barrett gives a very detailed definition of an African independent Church. He writes that 'independency' is

the formation and existence within a tribe or tribal unit, temporarily or permanently, of any organized religious movement with a distinct name and membership, even as small as a single organized congregation, which claims the title Christian in that it acknowledges Jesus Christ as Lord, and which has either separated by secession from a mission

---

1. The numbers are from 1967.

Church or an existing African independent Church, or has been founded outside the mission Churches as a new kind of religious entity under African initiative and leadership.

(Barrett 1968: 50)

An African independent Church is, then, a Church that has been founded under African initiative, in most cases by secession from an already existing Church, either a mission Church or another independent one. And, to be counted as an African independent Church, it must be recognizable as a Church, that is, it must acknowledge Jesus Christ as Lord.

A number of books have been written about the African independent Churches, many of them analysing the reasons why these Churches have come into existence. There appears to be general agreement among many writers that independent Churches have arisen in response to a social situation in which people feel insecure or deprived of the riches they see others having. Against this background, these Churches are interpreted as a kind of protest movement. The people who become members of them have not had the incentive to let their dissatisfaction be expressed through violent means. But that they form independent Churches nevertheless reflects their dissatisfaction, in that they choose to take up a passive attitude towards the society surrounding them and to form their own society, as far as possible in isolation from other people.[2]

In this book I not only analyse the basic causes of the formation of independent Churches, but also look at the reasons why so many people find them attractive and at the benefits they appear to derive from them. Welbourn points out that independent Churches are mostly small, intimate groups, whose members are able to experience a true fellowship with each other, and where each person is regarded as important. These are characteristics that are of great significance for people who live in a rapidly changing modern world in which the old fellowships have broken down, and in which individuals no longer receive their identities from their position in the clan or tribe. In this situation the

2. This theory is expressed by, among others, the following authors: Peel (1968), Ranger (1968: 437–53, 631–41) and Welbourn (1961). The same theory applies to Melanesia, according to Worsley (1968).

independent Church becomes 'a place [in which] to feel at home' (Welbourn and Ogot 1966). A number of writers emphasize the importance of the leadership positions offered by the independent Churches to people who would otherwise have no possibility of exercising their abilities as leaders (Sangree 1966: xxx; Sundkler 1970: 100).

When evaluating the theological beliefs of African independent Churches, writers disagree about whether or not they can be recognized as truly Christian. Beyerhaus finds that Jesus Christ is not regarded by them as the central figure in their faith, but that they emphasize the Holy Spirit at the expense of Jesus. He finds also that their soteriology is not Christian in that they do not emphasize salvation from sin, but rather delivery from the evil powers they see as a threat to human life. He cannot therefore regard them as truly Christian. His characterization of the independent Churches is that Christianity has provided their outward form, but that the traditional African religion is responsible for the interpretation of their beliefs, and cultural changes determine their practical aims (Beyerhaus 1967). Sundkler, on the other hand, has revised his opinion on the question of whether these Churches are Christian or syncretistic. His conclusion in the first edition of his book *Bantu Prophets in South Africa* was that, 'The syncretistic sect becomes the bridge over which Africans are brought back to heathenism' (Sundkler 1970: 297). But in the second edition of the same book he says that this viewpoint was probably too Western, because the people who are members of independent Churches regard them as definitely Christian organizations, 'adapted to their own real needs', and as 'bridges to a new and richer experience of life' (Sundkler 1970: 297). Turner says that the criteria for judging whether or not an independent Church may be regarded as truly Christian must be its acceptance of the Scriptures and its sharing in the mission and service of Christ to men. He is willing to recognize a group as a Christian Church if it conforms to these criteria, even if it may not have grasped the full significance of Christ (Turner 1967b: 332).

1. History of the Holy Spirit Movement

Friends Africa Mission before 1927

Arrival of the First Missionaries

Three young Quakers, Willis R. Hotchkiss, Arthur B. Chilson and Edgar T. Hole, were among the first missionaries from overseas to arrive in western Kenya. They came to what was then called North Kavirondo District in 1902 (Painter 1966: 20). This district covered approximately the area of the present Western Province, which is inhabited by the various Abaluyia tribes.

Missionary work in what is now Kenya had already started by the middle of the nineteenth century. The first missionaries were German Lutherans, Ludwig Krapf and Johann Rebmann, who were sent out by the British Church Missionary Society. Krapf arrived on the coast near Mombasa in 1844 and Rebmann joined him two years later. They were unable to penetrate far into the country, so their work was limited to a few settlements for freed slaves at the coast (Oliver 1967: 6).

Europeans did not go far inland during the nineteenth century because they feared the Masai people, whom they believed to be very warlike and hostile to any foreigners who went into their area. However, in the 1890s the British government became interested in maintaining permanent links with the kingdom of Buganda and, for this purpose, needed to keep the peace along the direct caravan route which went through what is now Kenya. During the last few years of the century British troops consequently carried out wars of 'pacification' against the tribes living between the Indian Ocean and Uganda. These people were now forced to submit to British authority and to allow foreigners to travel freely (Ingham 1966: 171; Rosberg and Nottingham 1966: 7). This new situation opened up opportunities for Christian missionaries who would now be able to travel inland without fear of being attacked by unfriendly tribes. From around the turn of the century several missionary societies sent out pioneer missionaries who explored the country and found the sites where they were to establish their mission stations. Those that decided to work in North Kavirondo were the Friends Africa Industrial Mission, the Church of God, the Anglican Church Missionary Society and the Roman Catholic Mill Hill Mission. All four of these societies came into the area before 1905; a few years later they were joined by the Pentecostal Assemblies of Canada (Oliver 1967: 170).

The Friends Africa Industrial Mission was created by American Quakers in 1901.[1] When Willis Hotchkiss returned to the Friends Bible Training School in Cleveland, Ohio, after having spent four years (from 1895) with missionaries of the Africa Inland Mission in British East Africa, as Kenya was then called, he felt that the Friends should start a mission in that country. The Friends in Cleveland readily accepted his proposal (Painter 1966: 20).

The establishment of this missionary society had its background in the evangelical revival which had taken place among American Quakers in the Midwest during the nineteenth century. The majority of Friends in this area now adhered to the general evangelical belief in the importance of saving man's sinful soul. The original Quaker principle of the Inner Light, namely the indwelling of the Divine Spirit in every man, was regarded as heresy. Consequently, these American Quakers, like many other evangelical Protestants in Europe and North America, felt they ought to bring the Christian gospel of God's forgiveness through the death of Jesus Christ to non-Christians (Kay 1973: 51). So when Hotchkiss came home and spoke of the need he had found for a mission in British East Africa, the Friends in Cleveland responded immediately by organizing the Friends Africa Industrial Mission.[2]

When the first three missionaries from this society reached Kenya in 1902, they had no specific idea about where in the country they wanted to establish their mission, but believed that

1. The names 'Friends' and 'Quakers' refer to the same Church and are used synonymously.
2. The name was later changed to Friends Africa Mission.

'under Divine leading their course would be made clear' (Painter 1966: 21). They went by train along the newly constructed railway line from Mombasa to Kisumu, and here they were helped by the British district commissioner, C. W. Hobley, to get acquainted with the North Kavirondo area. After some travels they came in October to Kaimosi, the place where they decided to build their mission station. At first they camped there because both Hole and Hotchkiss had become ill. But they soon discovered that the place was ideally suited for the kind of mission they wanted to establish (Painter 1966: 21).

In their first mission report in 1903 the missionaries in Kaimosi outlined the purpose they wanted the Friends Africa Industrial Mission to serve:

> The primary object of Friends Africa Industrial Mission is the evangelization of the heathen. The industrial Feature is introduced into the work for the purpose of exerting continuous Christian influence over the natives employed, with the hope of obtaining the following results: Teaching them habits of industry and ultimately establishing a self-supporting native Christian Church.
>
> (Painter 1966: 24)

Like many other missionaries, these Quakers believed that preaching the gospel of Christ was in itself not enough. For Africans to become truly Christian, it was also necessary to teach them many aspects of the Western way of life. Alta Hoyt, a missionary in Kaimosi from 1912 until 1945 (Painter 1966: 143), wrote that it is necessary to teach Africans the love of God first so that they may accept Christ as their personal saviour, 'and in order to grow as Christians they must learn to read, teach and develop along all lines' (Hoyt 1971: 31).

The first three missionaries found Kaimosi an ideal place in which to realize their vision of an industrial mission. Here they found the falls of the Goli Goli river, which could be used for water power. There was a big forest that could supply wood for a sawmill. The land was fertile and would make it possible to grow crops in the mission. And the altitude, 5500 feet above sea level, made the climate well suited for the American missionaries. With the help of the district commissioner the missionaries acquired

1000 acres of land at Kaimosi, and here they began to build their mission station (Painter 1966: 22).

As soon as they had decided to settle at Kaimosi, the missionaries began their evangelizing mission. From the beginning they held services for worship every Sunday, to which people came from the surrounding villages. Every morning all the workers on the mission compound came together for a short service of Bible reading, prayer and singing.

The industrial work was also started immediately. As soon as possible a dam was built across the Goli Goli river and a watermill was erected, which was used for sawing timber and grinding grain. Forest was cleared, crops were planted and many houses were built at the mission.

Medical ministry was regarded as an important aid in spreading the gospel. When a doctor arrived from America in 1903, he started a small dispensary at Kaimosi, and he also went out to the villages to treat people near to their homes.

But the educational work was what proved most helpful in bringing converts to the mission. The missionaries started an educational programme less than half a year after their arrival at Kaimosi. Their aim was to give Africans sufficient education to become leaders in local congregations, so that through them the gospel could be spread more effectively. Also, education was seen as an important factor in the 'development' of the Africans. The content of this missionary education weighed heavily in favour of religious instruction, but the pupils also learnt reading, writing and arithmetic. The pupils from the first school at Kaimosi went out to their villages as teachers and, within a few years, many small schools had been started along the same lines as the school at the mission station (Painter 1966: 24).

Within a few years of the arrival of the first three missionaries in 1902, the Friends Africa Industrial Mission had laid the foundations of its future work in the fields of evangelization, industry, medicine and education. At first only a small number of converts were won, but the changes brought about by the colonial administration were soon to make more people come to the mission to seek the benefits of the new religion and of education.

The Colonial Setting

In 1894 the British declared the kingdom of Buganda, together with some other areas, a protectorate, namely the Protectorate of Uganda. The eastern part of this protectorate was the area that is now western Kenya. Here they placed an administrative post at Mumias, the capital of the Wanga tribe (Ingham 1966: 151; Were 1967: 155).[3] At that time North Kavirondo was of interest to the British only as a caravan route on the way to Buganda and as a supply area. However, to secure the caravan route it was necessary for them to control the people of the area. This they wanted to do through chiefs who were to be responsible for the maintenance of peace. But most Abaluyia tribes had no chiefs at the time of the arrival of the British. The largest social unit under normal circumstances was the clan, and the highest authority in the running of its affairs was the clan head. The only tribe that was united under a chief was the Wanga, who were ruled by Chief Mumia. So when the British wanted to carry through their policy of 'indirect rule' they had to create chiefs in most places. Those clans that claimed a genealogical relationship with each other were united to form a tribal unit, and each such tribe was brought under the authority of a chief. In places where no suitable chief could be found, the British made use of Wanga supporters of Mumia, who were installed as chiefs over these other tribes. Mumia himself was appointed paramount chief over all the Abaluyia in 1909, and he held this post until his retirement in 1926 (Lonsdale 1964: 21, 92; Were 1967: 172).

Peace was now secured in North Kavirondo. But soon the British made their authority over the area more clearly felt. In 1901 the railway line from Mombasa to Kisumu was completed. Originally it was started in order to make communications with Buganda easier. But once it had been constructed, the British wanted to bring the area through which it passed under more effective control. And in the year 1900 they confirmed their authority by starting to collect hut tax with the help of the newly installed chiefs (Lonsdale 1964: 81).

In 1902 the Kavirondo area was transferred from the Protectorate of Uganda to the East Africa Protectorate, the area which was in 1920 to become Kenya Colony, and here it became the

---

3. The administrative centre was moved to Kakamega in 1920.

Province of Nyanza (Rosberg and Nottingham 1966: 58). When European settlers arrived in the East Africa Protectorate soon after the completion of the railway, Nyanza, of which the northern part was North Kavirondo District, was to become an important source of labour for the European farms. This supply of labour had been facilitated through the transfer of the province from Uganda.

From 1912, when the Native Authority Ordinance was introduced, the chiefs were given wide powers to 'encourage' people to seek labour outside their 'reserves', as the tribal areas were now called. Many people were keen to work for European farmers, for this gave them an opportunity to save money for bridewealth or for buying some of the new things introduced by the Europeans, for instance bicycles. Also, many had to seek wage labour to be able to pay the taxes imposed by the British administration (Lonsdale 1964: 11). When the voluntary supply of labour failed to keep pace with the settlers' demands, the chiefs were able to use their own powers to coerce their people into seeking work on the farms.

The chiefs were also obliged to recruit people to perform unpaid labour for the government, especially to construct roads. In addition, they had to encourage people to plant new crops, such as cotton and beans, and maintain law and order by arresting wrongdoers and by presiding over the locational tribunal for the trial of minor cases. And they were responsible for collecting taxes within their respective locations (Lonsdale 1964: 166).

The coming of the First World War increased the demand for manpower from North Kavirondo District. The British troops needed Africans as porters in the Carrier Corps, and the number of men conscripted for this work was very large. The district commissioner for North Kavirondo reported that in 1914–15 the number registered for Carrier Corps work was 4372. This number grew during the following years and in 1917–18 as many as 10,036 men were registered (North Kavirondo District 1917). When these figures are compared with the number of men in the district, which in 1923 was reported to be 84,889 (North Kavirondo District 1923), it will be seen that a large proportion of the male population had to leave the area and become porters.

After the First World War, in 1919, the British administration introduced a registration system for all African men over 16 years of age. People who wanted to leave their reserve to work had to carry a registration card, *kipande*, at all times. This system was introduced to make it easier for the authorities to control the movement of people and to catch those who deserted their work in the white areas (Rosberg and Nottingham 1966: 45).

In 1920 the East Africa Protectorate changed its status and became a British colony, now called Kenya. In many parts of the country this change revived the fear among Africans that white settlers would take over an even larger part of African land than they had already done (Rosberg and Nottingham 1966: 58). Though no land alienation had taken place so far in North Kavirondo, the fear for the security of the tribal land was always present. In 1931 this fear was to prove well-founded when gold was found near Kakamega. The previous year a law had been passed which guaranteed that the land in the reserves should belong to the Africans for ever, but the discovery of gold made the government ignore this law and a densely populated area was cleared of its inhabitants to make space for the European gold-diggers (Lonsdale 1970: 620).

Thus, from around the turn of the century until the beginning of the 1930s the British made their presence in North Kavirondo felt in very many ways. The clan was supplanted by the tribe as the most important political unit and the traditional clan heads lost their power. Instead, official chiefs were installed to carry out the wishes of the British, and the changes introduced through them were so extensive that the people's everyday lives were seriously affected. The conscription of men for the Carrier Corps during the First World War and the alienation of land when gold was discovered at Kakamega in 1931 further affected the Abaluyia people. Attempts were made by the Africans to form political protest movements. In 1924 the North Kavirondo Taxpayers' Welfare Association was formed among members of the Church Missionary Society. And in 1932 another group of people, mostly adherents of the Friends Africa Mission, set up the North Kavirondo Central Association (Lonsdale 1970: 618).

The majority of the members of these organizations were people who had been educated at mission schools. The missionaries had by now been able to win many converts, and the education that was given at their schools had come to play an important role in the development of Abaluyia society.

The Response to the Missionaries' Teaching

In his book *The Missionary Factor in East Africa*, Roland Oliver says that the second phase of missionary activity, the first few years after mission stations had been established in the interior of the country, was not basically different from the first phase, when mission was limited to settlements for freed slaves at the coast. The difference consisted only in 'the number of points occupied'. The fundamental problem, that only those who had in one way or another been separated from their tribal society responded to the missionaries' teachings, existed even during this second phase (Oliver 1967: 172).

At the Friends Africa Industrial Mission the first five converts were received into Church membership in 1905. These were all young people who had left their normal surroundings to be employed in the homes of missionaries. The response among people living under normal circumstances in their tribes was very limited. In 1906 five more people were converted to Christianity, and in 1907 one person joined the mission. In 1911 the number of African Christians was still only 16 (Painter 1966: 32).

Attendance at Sunday worship services was, however, much higher than the number of converts. An important reason for this was that the official chiefs were under government orders to assist the missionaries. So when messages were sent out to the villages from the mission inviting chiefs to bring their people for worship, the response was good. In some cases the chiefs even used force to make their people attend the services (Kay 1973: 108; Painter 1966: 28).

Voluntary interest in mission activities grew after the government had firmly established its system of official chiefs around 1906. These chiefs soon realized how important education would become in the carrying out of their official duties. And the only source of education was the mission stations. So when the missionaries of the Friends Africa Industrial Mission appealed to them to send their sons and subjects to the mission schools, they did so eagerly so that their sons would receive the education necessary to succeed them as chiefs (Kay 1973: 91).

The young people themselves also realized that education could open up new opportunities for them within the colonial system. The young men could no longer perform their traditional role as tribal warriors, but saw that they might play an important role in the modern society if they made use of the educational facilities provided by the missionaries (Kay 1973: 116).

Because of this interest in education shown by both the chiefs and the young people, the Friends school system proved to be one of the most important means through which the missionaries could spread their message. The education given in the Friends schools was centred on teaching the pupils about Christianity. Other subjects were also taught, but were often linked to religious instruction. For example, reading lessons frequently consisted of reading Bible stories. Because of this, the Africans came to look upon education and Christianity as closely interrelated (Painter 1966: 55).

The spread of Friends schools to the villages therefore soon began to bring converts to the mission. Painter reports that in 1914, when the school system had been in operation for some years, a major breakthrough occurred. In that year 35 persons were received into membership, more than doubling the previous number of members. And from that year the membership grew steadily (Painter 1966: 35).

The school system was one factor, and a very important one, in bringing about the conversion of the Abaluyia people to Christianity. But it was not the only factor. Oliver says that not until society had changed to such an extent that the traditional authorities had lost their power and people had got connections beyond their own tribes did mass conversion to Christianity occur. The traditional religion came to be considered inadequate in the new situation, while the religion brought by the missionaries was seen as one that could give a feeling of security in the modern society (Oliver 1967: 198).

Abaluyia society had experienced many changes during the first years of colonial rule. The lives of everybody had been affected through taxation, wage labour away from home, forced labour on roads, the planting of new crops, the new authority system and modern education. Under the old authority system the clan head was seen as the mediator between the clan ancestors and the members of the clan, and his authority derived from the sanction of the ancestors (Lonsdale 1964: 21). Now a system had been introduced under which those in official positions had no traditional religious sanction for their power. The many other changes that occurred under the colonial government had helped towards the disintegration of the traditional world view. Many people had been outside their tribal areas as labourers on European farms, and later as porters during the war. When they came home they would often regard the tribal society as too limited and its religion as inadequate for the larger society they had experienced.

The insecurity created by all these changes, coupled with the breakdown of the authority of the old religion, made many people turn to Christianity. They saw colonial administrators and missionaries cooperating in many ways. And since the traditional Abaluyia world view made no distinction between secular and religious spheres in life, most people viewed European society in the same way (Welbourn and Ogot 1966: 117). Christianity was regarded as the religion that would be able to give the same security in the new society as the traditional religion had given in the old.

All missions in western Kenya experienced a great influx of new converts after the First World War (Lonsdale 1964: 212). The Friends Africa Mission, which in 1914 had 60 members, could in 1920 report a membership of 351, with an additional 682 persons in training for membership (Painter 1966: 35, 38). By now the mission had established five stations. The original station at Kaimosi in Tiriki location continued to be the centre of missionary activity. But already in 1906 a station had been set up at Vihiga in south Maragoli and another at Lirhanda in Isukha location. In 1915 a station was opened at Lugulu in Kitosh, and in 1919 one was established at Malava in Kabras location. All these stations could report a growing number of members. The area that responded best to the missionaries' teachings was Maragoli, followed by Isukha and Idakho (Painter 1966: 30).

Maragoli was already densely populated, so when locational boundaries were fixed the population pressure was such that the disintegration of the traditional society was felt earlier here than in other areas. Before the coming of the colonial administration, it had always been possible for people to leave densely populated areas. A lineage could break off from its parent lineage and find land somewhere else (Wagner 1949: 57). Because this outlet was closed when the new administrators laid down fixed boundaries for each location, the new opportunities opened up by wage labour and education were seized eagerly when the pressure on land made traditional agriculture less profitable (Kay 1973: 123).

In Isukha and Idakho the pressure on land was not as great as in Maragoli. In 1923 north Maragoli had a population of 697 per square mile while the number in south Maragoli was 364. In comparison, west Kakamega (Idakho) had 162 persons per square mile, and east Kakamega (Isukha) only 93 (North Kavirondo District 1923). The social changes brought about by the colonial government were also felt here, though not to quite the same extent as in Maragoli. Also, the Friends Africa Mission had started work here at an early date, already in 1906, strongly supported by the chief, Ichivini (Kay 1973: 109). This long involvement of the mission, combined with the needs created by changes in society, made many people in the area convert to Christianity. In 1920 the membership here was 62, with 160 persons attending classes before becoming full members (Painter 1966: 38).

Membership of the Friends Africa Mission grew steadily during the 1920s and, at its peak in 1932, it was reported as high as 9408 (Kay 1973: 166). The social changes introduced by the colonial administration had destroyed the traditional society and given people a feeling of insecurity. The Christianity the missionaries had brought was looked upon as the religion of the new society and therefore as the religion able to reintegrate society. Education at mission schools, which was seen as an aspect of Christianity, had proved to be one of the most important aids towards advancement in the new society. Therefore, to benefit from both the spiritual and material aspects of the new order, many people had responded positively to the missionaries' teachings and had become converted to Christianity. But after the membership of the Friends Africa Mission reached a peak in 1932, it plunged suddenly over the next two years. More than 2000 people left the mission, a large part of them to join the Holy Spirit movement. In 1934 the membership of the mission was only 7048 (Kay 1973: 166).

Outpouring of the Holy Spirit in 1927

The Influence of Arthur Chilson
In September 1927 there was a yearly meeting of the Friends Africa Mission at Kaimosi. Arthur Chilson, the missionary in charge of the meeting, decided to deliver the message of Pentecost to the people assembled there. He told them that to be a true

Christian required baptism with the Holy Spirit and that to receive this baptism it was necessary to confess all one's sins openly and to pray for forgiveness. His message strongly affected his listeners. They knelt down, they confessed and asked God to forgive their sins. When this had been going on for some time, Arthur Chilson stood up and lifted his hands over the heads of the congregation. He prayed that they might receive the baptism with the Holy Spirit. The meeting was now seized by the Spirit. People were crying, everything was shaking, and many began to speak in tongues. To show them the biblical authority for what they had just experienced, Chilson read Acts 2:1–4:

> When the day of Pentecost had come, they were all together in one place. And suddenly a sound came from heaven like the rush of a mighty wind, and it filled all the house where they were sitting. And there appeared to them tongues as of fire, distributed and resting on each one of them. And they were all filled with the Holy Spirit and began to speak in other tongues, as the Spirit gave them utterance.[4]

He pointed out that when they shook and spoke in tongues they were influenced by the same power of the Holy Spirit which had seized the disciples of Jesus on the day of Pentecost (Mavuru and Ihaji 1975; interview with Kefa Ayub Mavura, 24 January 1975).

Chilson did not stop his preaching about the baptism with the Holy Spirit after the yearly meeting. At this time he was a teacher of religion for a group of 20 pupils at the school at Kaimosi. His message to them was the same as the one he had preached at the yearly meeting: that unless they repented all their sins, confessed them openly and prayed earnestly to God for forgiveness, they would be unable to receive the Holy Spirit. Their sinfulness was like a lid that covered them so that they were not open to receive the gift of the Holy Spirit. Although they regarded themselves as Christians, they were not saved; they only believed in God. Unless they were baptized with the Holy Spirit their salvation was not a true one, and they could have no assurance of going to heaven. His pupils responded strongly, just as the congregation at the yearly meeting had done. They began to confess their sins openly

4. I quote from the Revised Standard Version of the English Bible.

to each other, and when Chilson prayed for them they received the Holy Spirit. This happened in October 1927 (speech by Japhet Zale Ambula during Holy Spirit Church of East Africa service at Bukoyani headquarters, 18 January 1975; interview with him, 16 June 1975).

The people who had experienced the outpouring of the Holy Spirit in Kaimosi did not keep their new experience to themselves. When they went home from the yearly meeting they preached to the Church members in their villages about the baptism with the Holy Spirit. They taught them what they had learnt from Chilson, that it was necessary first to repent and confess one's sins openly and to pray to God for forgiveness before one could receive the Holy Spirit. The pupils who had been taught by Chilson did the same when they came home to their villages, and the response was strong. Soon a number of the village congregations of the Friends Africa Mission were affected by the new revival (interviews with Kefa Ayub Mavuru, 24 January 1975, and Japhet Zale Ambula, 16 June 1975).

The person who had started this revival was Arthur Chilson, and he had done it purposely. He and his wife had been praying for a Holy Spirit revival for years before 1927. They strongly believed that even though hundreds of people had accepted the belief in Jesus Christ, they still needed the baptism with the Holy Spirit (Chilson 1943: 165).

Chilson's conviction of the necessity of the baptism with the Holy Spirit originated in his own experience. He had been personally involved in the revival movement in America in the late nineteenth century. One branch of this revival, which made a strong impact on many Quaker congregations in the Midwest, had a Pentecostal touch to it in that it professed a two-stage way to salvation. To be saved a person had to be justified, and this justification would come as God's response when the person had confessed his sins and declared his faith in Jesus Christ. But after this first stage some people reached a second and higher stage of salvation: sanctification. Justification was salvation because of God's grace. But it did not change the person's tendency to sin. Sanctification, on the other hand, meant a conversion of the heart worked by the Holy Spirit. It did not take away man's sinful nature, but it made it possible through the power of the Holy Spirit to resist temptation. This second stage of salvation was often accompanied by an outpouring of the Holy Spirit (Kay 1973: 56. For a description of the belief in sanctification among Pentecostals, see Hollenweger 1972: 21).

Arthur Chilson had the experience of being converted and receiving justification when he was about 16 years old. But around 1892, approximately four years later, he entered a second spiritual crisis. He prayed together with his pastor and now 'he saw that there was complete victory for him when he was sanctified and baptized with the Holy Ghost'. This insight meant that he 'laid his all on the altar', after which he 'received the blessed Holy Ghost in all His fullness' (Chilson 1943: 1).

When he came to Kenya as a missionary, Chilson became one of the most important preachers of the Friends Africa Mission. Within a year of his arrival he was already holding meetings at various points outside the mission station at Kaimosi. He was always eager to expand the mission work into new areas and Painter (1966: 23, 37) describes him as a 'magnetic and challenging' preacher. He did not wait long before he began to teach about receiving the Holy Spirit. Already in 1909, when the number of members of the mission was still only eleven (Painter 1966: 35), his wife reports that they held Sunday afternoon meetings for members only, and here 'We have felt led to give special lessons on the baptism with the Holy Ghost' (Chilson 1943: 84).

But it was not until 1924 that this message began to meet with any greater response among the Africans. At the Native Prayer Conference in that year Chilson's sermons stirred the people into making confessions, and some said that his message made their hearts quake (Chilson 1943: 156). This was at Malava where the Chilson family were now staying. During the same conference the following year Chilson again preached about the baptism with the Holy Spirit and reported that 'a number very definitely and intelligently began seeking the baptism with the Holy Ghost' (Chilson 1925).

The breakthrough came in 1926. The *Report of the Native Affairs Committee* of that year says, 'At the Native Prayer Conference, the prayers of years were answered and we had a real visitation from the Lord. Many confessed and found pardon for sin; many sought and received the baptism with the Holy Ghost.' But although the revival seems to have started in 1926, it was not until 1927 that the outpouring of the Holy Spirit was to have such an effect on people that it spread from Kaimosi out to the village congregations of the Friends Church.

A factor that probably contributed to the great effect of Chilson's preaching in 1927 was that towards the end of 1926 the Chilson family moved from Malava to Kaimosi, because Jefferson Ford, another important preacher, went home on furlough (*Minutes*, 18 October 1926). Before, Chilson had brought his message of the baptism with the Holy Spirit to the comparatively new congregation in Kabras. Now he was preaching at the original mission station, and the people who came together for the annual conference here had been under the influence of the Friends Africa Mission for longer than the people at Malava. Many of them came from Maragoli, the area that had responded most positively to the missionaries' teachings, and also from Isukha and Idakho where the Friends had established their work as early as 1906. Many of these people had been Christians for a number of years. Their contact with the missionaries was of longer standing than was the case further north, and they had therefore also experienced more of the strains that could develop through this relationship. Many had been educated at the Friends schools, and they had now reached a level of maturity in their dealings with the missionaries that made them seek more independence from their supervision. When Chilson preached at Kaimosi, his listeners were therefore more critical of traditional missionary teachings than those at Malava, and at the same time more receptive to new teachings that might seem to bring them a measure of independence from the missionaries.

Chilson himself looked upon the outpouring of the Holy Spirit in Kaimosi in 1927 as the revival for which he had prayed for years. He writes (Chilson 1927): 'We have seen wonderful answers to prayer. We have been privileged to attend some of the most powerful Spiritual meetings in all our experience.' But in the same report he complains:

Had the Mission been adequately supported by the right type of workers sent out and sufficient finances, we could have had the most wonderful Spiritual awakening this past year among the natives of these districts ever experienced by a Mission in Africa and while there has been most blessed work by the Holy Ghost among old and young, I am convinced that thousands could have been brought into the fold could we but have taken advantage of the opportunity.

He found that the revival he had started had not reached sufficient people, and he attributed this limitation to a lack of missionary staff.

Chilson may not have foreseen how many people would become affected by the Holy Spirit revival after 1927. He did not stay to watch the results of his preaching. In January 1928 he left Kaimosi and did not return to his work there (Chilson 1943: 169). His complaint that there were not enough missionaries to take care of the continuation of the work reflects the situation in which the Friends Africa Mission found itself in the late 1920s. A number of missionaries retired and went home, but no replacement was sent from America (Painter 1966: 65). The situation was so serious that the district commissioner found it necessary to write about it to the provincial commissioner in Kisumu. In 1930 he described in a letter how Mr Ford tried to cover the supervision of all the Friends mission stations, and he expressed his fear that the African Christians would get out of hand for the missionaries and begin to create disturbances (North Kavirondo District 1930).

Events in the years following 1927 proved that the situation had indeed become uncontrollable for the missionaries. The revival for which Arthur Chilson had prayed and worked spread through the preaching of African Christians to a large number of local congregations. His wish had been that there should be an outpouring of the Holy Spirit on members of the Friends Africa Mission, so that the Church would experience a spiritual renewal. But when he left, other missionaries took over the task of guiding the revival into the right channels. These missionaries did not share Chilson's views on the desirability of the baptism with the Holy Spirit. With the help of their supporters among the African Christians they tried to calm down the noisy manifestations of the Holy Spirit. But they did not succeed, and eventually the conflict between their repressive attitude and the persistence of those people who had received the Holy Spirit led to a split.

Movement of the Spirit in Friends Meetings
The Holy Spirit revival had been started by a missionary, but his message of baptism with the Spirit after repentance and confession

of all sins was received eagerly by the African Christians. Through their preaching, the revival spread from Kaimosi out to village meetings of the Friends Church.

The area where the Friends Africa Mission had met with the greatest response to its teachings was Maragoli. And it was also Maragoli that was soon to become a stronghold of the Holy Spirit people. Daniel Mundia was one of those students at Kaimosi who had received the Holy Spirit under the guidance of Arthur Chilson, and he went from there to his home area in south Maragoli to preach the new message. Here he taught that if people had sinned it was not enough just to pray. To be forgiven they would have to confess all their sins openly. When they had confessed everything they would be cleansed of their sins, and would now be open to receive the Holy Spirit.

Daniel Mundia went back to school at Kaimosi. But the message he had preached had come to receptive hearts. One of the monthly meeting[5] leaders was Jacob Buluku. He was greatly moved by Daniel's preaching, and when he went away Jacob continued to teach people about confessing and receiving the Holy Spirit. Soon all the villages around Vihiga had been affected by the revival.

On 6 January 1928 a monthly meeting was held at the Friends church at Vihiga. Hundreds of people were present, and there was much rejoicing and praising the Lord because they had now repented and been cleansed of all their sins. Both leaders and ordinary members joined each other in confessing all they had done and in thanking God for their new assurance of forgiveness.

But the fellowship in the Holy Spirit was soon to be disturbed. It was not long before the leading Church elders realized that what was going on in their Churches was out of keeping with the wishes of most missionaries of the Friends Africa Mission. Japhet Zale Ambula, the present archbishop of the Holy Spirit Church of East Africa, describes what happened in this way: 'Satan does not sleep. Because Satan realized that he had been judged he went through to only six senior Church elders. Then they were so ashamed.' They were ashamed because people confessed all kinds of sins publicly, even serious offences like adultery or stealing. They tried to teach

---

5. In Quaker terminology the word 'meeting' means both a gathering of people and the organizational set-up of the gathering.

their members again what the missionaries used to say, that 'if people have sinned you shall only pray and pray, then you will be forgiven.'

The first step taken by these elders was to form a committee and to call the 20 boys who had been baptized with the Holy Spirit in Kaimosi in front of the committee. The boys were told that the message they had been spreading was a shameful one and that it had been rejected by the leadership of the Friends Church. If they continued to preach about the Holy Spirit they would have to leave the Friends schools. Since all schools in that area were controlled by the Friends Africa Mission this was a strong threat, and it made a number of them leave the Holy Spirit movement.

These elders spoke in all their congregations against the public confessions and the noisy manifestations of the Holy Spirit. They tried to threaten people into giving up their new ways, and many were influenced by them to the extent that they returned to the accepted customs of the Friends Church. But two village congregations remained faithful to their experience of the Holy Spirit. They were Bukoyani and Muhanda. Bukoyani was the village in which Jacob Buluku was now staying, and at Muhanda was another important follower of the Holy Spirit movement, Daniel Sande. These two men were to emerge as the leaders of the Holy Spirit people in south Maragoli.

When in 1929 the Friends' elders had not succeeded in threatening the people from Bukoyani and Muhanda into giving up their open confessions and their belief in the outpouring of the Holy Spirit, they called them in front of their committee. Here they were told that the spirit they had was a bad one, and that if they would not give up their confessions and their shouting and speaking in tongues, they would be expelled from the Friends Africa Mission. Jacob Buluku now stood up as the spokesman of the Holy Spirit people. He answered the elders that if the spirit which had seized them had been a bad one it would not have revealed all people's sins, and he refused to return to the old customs of the Friends. The elders then said that if they persisted, their names would be deleted from the mission's membership book. To this Jacob replied, 'Then take them out. Our names are written in the book in heaven.'

For the Holy Spirit people in south Maragoli, this was the decisive split from the Friends Africa Mission. The committee elders told them to leave the Church, and they went out singing song no. 57 in the Friends' Luragoli hymn book, especially v.4 which says:

> Lwa ndihirwa mu shirwadzo,
> Mwoyo gwanje nemirembe
> Nindi nobulunji bwebwe,
> Nunu nyenya Yesu mwene.

English translation:

> When I will be sent before the court,
> My heart will be in peace
> When I have His righteousness,
> Now I want Jesus himself.

They were sure that their choice was the right one. After confession of all their sins they had received the baptism with the Holy Spirit. They felt that they had seen God himself (Japhet Zale Ambula in a speech during a church service at the Bukoyani headquarters of the Holy Spirit Church of East Africa, 18 January 1975) and received His righteousness, and therefore they had no reason to fear human persecution.

The split was final. The Holy Spirit people refused to give up what they saw as the truth. And the Friends' elders were unwilling to accommodate such views and practices in their Church. The committee members sent messages out to all Friends meetings, saying that these people had been expelled from the Friends Africa Mission. No other congregation should receive them, and if they were seen in any of the Friends churches, they ought to be sent away (description based on interview with Japhet Zale Ambula, 16 June 1975).

In north Maragoli much the same thing happened. Here again, the message of the baptism with the Holy Spirit was spread by people who had attended the yearly meeting, or who had been to school under Arthur Chilson at Kaimosi. The first place in this area to be affected was the village of Endeli. A woman here, Enis Kadali, received the Holy Spirit in 1927, and she soon got other people involved in the revival. Joseph Chegero, who was to become a leading figure in the Holy Spirit movement in north

Maragoli, was converted in the same year when she and two others went to his house and began to pray in the Spirit. Enis's husband, Daudi Sagida Ludundu, also joined the movement and soon a large number of people came together at Endeli, worshipping in the Holy Spirit.

As in south Maragoli, most of these people had previously belonged to the Friends Africa Mission. Joseph Chegero had been one of the elders of the village church. But when they began to confess openly and to shout and pray in the Holy Spirit they were soon forced to leave the Friends Church. For a few years the Friends tried to discipline them and even went so far as to beat them in an attempt to bring them back to accepted Church customs. But the Holy Spirit people were not defeated. What they were now experiencing was so much stronger than anything they had seen before, and they could not be persuaded to give it up. Thomas Malongo, who is now a member of the Gospel Holy Spirit of East Africa, describes (in an interview on 9 May 1975) the contrast between the ordinary missionary teachings and their new experience in this way:

> Ford and Rees [missionaries] did not teach people about the Holy Spirit, only the Ten Commandments, the dry message from the Bible without the Spirit. But ... God sent Chilson from Europe to teach the word of the Spirit. He taught them to kneel and pray. Then the Holy Spirit came to Kaimosi. When the Holy Spirit had come into the mind of members it became so sharp that they began to fight.

When the Holy Spirit came into people it was 'sharp' in contrast to the message people had heard from the missionaries before. This was regarded as a 'dry', dull message. Now they had the experience of being personally involved in Christian living through confession, praying and receiving the Holy Spirit. They were not to go back, even if their persistence meant that there would be conflict with the Friends Church. By 1930 it had come out into the open that the differences were irreparable, and they were now formally excluded from membership of the Friends Africa Mission (interviews with Elfas Ojiango Sagida, 1 March 1975, and Enis Kadali, 23 March 1975).

The third area in which the Holy Spirit movement was soon to become firmly established was Isukha and Idakho. Some of the people who had attended the yearly meeting at Kaimosi in 1927 came to this area to spread the news of the Holy Spirit revival; as in Maragoli, many members of the Friends Church readily accepted their message. But very soon the same conflict arose here as in the other places that had been affected by the revival. Those who received the Holy Spirit were to a large extent the less prominent people, ordinary members and the young. And as it happened in Maragoli, so it happened here: the Church elders soon realized that the majority of the missionaries were against the new teachings and most of them decided to follow the lead of the missionaries. They also made an attempt to cool down the other people who were seized by the Holy Spirit. At first they tried to use persuasion. When that failed to bring much result they began to beat the Holy Spirit people whenever they were assembled for worship (interview with Kefa Ayub Mavuru, 24 January 1975).

The people involved in the Holy Spirit movement soon developed a sense of fellowship, despite the distances between them. People in north and south Maragoli often visited each other to worship together, and those in Isukha and Idakho were also included in this fellowship. Archbishop Zale Ambula recalls how he and others from south Maragoli went to Isukha in 1932. Many people there had weakened in their fervour for the Holy Spirit because of the severe persecution by members of the Friends Church. So, to give them new courage and strength, those from south Maragoli came to visit them. When they were together one night, having a meeting in a private house, they suddenly saw a large group of Friends approaching. The Friends broke into the house where they were meeting and began to beat the Holy Spirit people. However, even such open acts of violence could not deter those who knew they had received the Holy Spirit. Despite the beatings Zale Ambula and the other visitors from south Maragoli stayed for a week and preached about the Holy Spirit, and a number of people were converted to their movement (interview with Japhet Zale Ambula, 13 January 1975).

Kefa Ayub Mavuru, who is now the high priest of the African Church of Holy Spirit, regards the conflict as having been between the Church elders and ordinary members. Though Jefferson Ford, the missionary most involved in evangelism after Arthur Chilson's departure, was not in favour of the loud manifestations of the

Holy Spirit, he still tried to reconcile the two groups in the Church. It was not the missionaries who stirred up people so that they beat others. The ones who did that were the African Church elders. However, they were not able to frighten everybody into going back to their old ways. A group of people persisted in their belief in the baptism with the Holy Spirit, and in November 1932 the final breaking point was reached. During the yearly meeting of the Friends Africa Mission at the Kitosh mission station in that month it was decided that all remaining adherents of the Holy Spirit movement must now be expelled from the Friends Church (interview with Kefa Ayub Mavuru, 24 January 1975).

The Holy Spirit movement had initially met with a very ready response from members of the Friends Africa Mission, especially in Maragoli, Isukha and Idakho. But when Church elders had seen the missionaries' negative attitude to this kind of movement they had soon reverted to their old style of worship. They had tried to bring others back with them, often through the use of threats, and many had followed their lead. But there still remained a group of Holy Spirit people who would not be threatened into giving up what they now saw as the truth from God. They had experienced a personal involvement in the Christian faith that was very different from their former much more passive acceptance of what the missionaries said, and they could not go back. Stirred into open persecution by their persistence, the Church elders began to break up Holy Spirit meetings, resorting to violence and beatings in their attempts to force them back. These elders had received their education through the Friends schools and were holding responsible positions in the Friends Church. They probably looked upon the new movement as a threat to their leadership. If they followed the example of the Holy Spirit people they would fall into disgrace with the missionaries and lose their positions in the Church. Consequently, those among them who had become involved in the Holy Spirit movement very soon gave up their involvement; they were prepared to use any means, even violence, to retain their leadership positions and their followers. When they finally realized that they would be unable to bring everybody back to their own ways, they denounced them altogether and expelled them from the Friends Church.

The Holy Spirit people had not thought of setting up their own Church; they regarded their movement as a revival within the

Friends Africa Mission. When they were expelled they therefore had no idea of how to organize a Church without missionaries and found themselves in a situation of uncertainty; their first reaction was to seek affiliation with other missions if possible. But most of them soon realized that they would have to find a way of living on their own. Since they had no one to tell them how to set up an independent Church, they withdrew from the world and isolated themselves while continuing with the style of worship they had learnt from the Holy Spirit. Gradually they came to see the way forward, and slowly a pattern of organization emerged which was to become the starting point for setting up independent Holy Spirit Churches.

Years of Isolation and Persecution

Isolation because of Social Tensions

When around 1930 the Holy Spirit people found themselves expelled from the Friends Africa Mission they were at a loss as to how to carry on with their movement. Only one independent African Church had by that time come into existence in Kenya. This was the Nomiya Luo Mission, which had been formed in 1914 after a split from the Anglican Church (Whisson 1964). But the Holy Spirit people were unlikely to have heard about this Church because it was in a different part of the country. The only kind of Churches they knew about were the mission Churches, which was why the idea of forming an independent Church did not occur to them sooner.

Another reason why they did not set up an independent Church organization during the first few years after the split is that those who were expelled had, for the most part, been ordinary members of the Friends Church. To retain their positions in the Church the majority of the leaders had very soon dissociated themselves from the Holy Spirit movement. The people who now found themselves without membership of any Church therefore had very little experience of church administration. There was nobody who could easily resume leadership and guide the others in establishing a new Church.

For these reasons, a good number of the Holy Spirit people soon made contact with the mission Churches that were more sympathetic to their ways of expressing religious sentiments than the Friends Africa Mission. This happened especially in south Maragoli, which was relatively close to the Pentecostal Assemblies of Canada in Nyang'ori and to the Salvation Army in Kisumu. In January 1932 the Holy Spirit followers from Bukoyani decided to attach themselves to the Pentecostal Church, where their loud praying and speaking in tongues could be accepted. Another group of Holy Spirit people in south Maragoli joined the Salvation Army, which, with its uniforms, banners and marching, proved to be attractive to them (interview with Japhet Zale Ambula, 13 January 1975).

In a letter to the commander of the Salvation Army in Nairobi, dated 1931, the missionaries of the Friends Africa Mission complained about the Salvation Army gaining adherents among people whom they considered to be followers of the Friends Church. They described them as being under discipline 'for certain fanatical activities', but expected them to 'yield to instruction' and rejoin the Friends Church. By now, however, they had contacted the Salvation Army captain in Kisumu and were about to become accepted as members of that Church (Salvation Army 1931).

The administrative officers were also concerned about what was happening. In 1931 the district commissioner reported that the Salvation Army was trying to start a 'hall' in south Maragoli among 'discontented Friends African [sic] Mission boys' (North Kavirondo District 1931). The following year the Salvation Army applied for permission to build a church, but was refused. The applicants now decided to build a church in spite of the refusal, and this led to proceedings against them (North Kavirondo District 1932). By 1934 matters had cooled down and the Salvation Army was 'winning an honourable place' (North Kavirondo District 1934). The Holy Spirit people who had joined them remained members of the Salvation Army.

The group that had attached itself to the Pentecostal Assemblies of Canada gave the administration more reason to worry. The district commissioner described these people as 'the less desirable elements of the Friends Mission', and he said (North Kavirondo District 1933) that the Nyang'ori mission had

educated them to a more emotional form of religeon [sic] and, this is the tragedy, failed in some instances to keep a grip on them. The result is that in south Maragoli two or three congregations have got quite out of hand, have been disowned by the Nyangori [sic] Mission and are practising a form of religeon [sic] of their own. The probability is that before long they will come in conflict with the law.

Japhet Zale Ambula claims that the Pentecostal mission did not disown them. After a year, in December 1932, the Holy Spirit people themselves decided to leave the mission. Nonetheless, at the beginning of 1933 the Bukoyani group found itself independent of any mission, and now had to find a way of continuing the Holy Spirit movement without any guidance from others.

The Pentecostal mission also gained some influence among the Holy Spirit people in other areas, and in Isukha and Idakho a number of them joined the Nyang'ori mission. Kefa Ayub Mavuru said (interview, 24 January 1975) that those were the people who were weak in faith and who did not trust the power of the Holy Spirit to lead them. Those who were strong remained unattached to any mission, even in the face of continuing persecution.

In this area the Holy Spirit movement gained in strength from around 1932. Kefa Ayub Mavuru himself joined this movement in 1955, and (he claimed in the same interview) so did many other former members of the Friends Church. The missionaries of the Friends Africa Mission reported in 1932 that there was a serious crisis in the Lirhanda branch of their Church. Eighteen people asked to have their names removed from the membership books of the mission so 'that they might be free to indulge in some fanatical costoms [sic] which they have adopted' (Native Affairs Committee 1932). And, as mentioned above, in November 1932 the mission decided to expel all Holy Spirit adherents in that area. The strengthening of the Holy Spirit movement in Isukha and Idakho from 1932 probably has to do with the discovery of gold around Kakamega in 1931 and the resulting alienation of what used to be African land. This introduced additional strains in a society already affected by the changes brought about by the colonial government.

Lonsdale (1964: 309) believes that the Friends missionaries' silence over the land alienation was partly responsible for leading people to join the Holy Spirit movement. He sees this movement as an expression of protest against the many changes introduced by the colonialists. The better-educated people voiced their protest

through political associations like the North Kavirondo Taxpayers' Welfare Association and the North Kavirondo Central
Association. The less educated members of society were unable to
articulate their grievances through such associations (Lonsdale
1964: 364), so instead 'sought to resolve the frustrations of the
colonial situation by shutting off secular political pressures'. Many
withdrew from active participation in the affairs of a society that
had changed so much that their normal way of life had been
seriously disrupted. The traditional religion had proved inadequate in dealing with this new situation, so Christianity became
the religion that would be able to reintegrate society. But
Christianity had been brought by Western missionaries who were
looked upon as the partners of the colonial administrators.
Through their educational system they served the colonial state,
and they were known to inform the government about what
happened among the African population. Also, the reintegration
of society sought through Christianity was hindered by the
missionaries' paternalistic attitude and practice of racial discrimination (Lonsdale 1964: 349). Protest against the colonial
situation would therefore often take the form of protest against
the missionaries. When people withdrew from society in passive
protest against the pressures brought to bear upon them in that
society they also withdrew from their association with the missionaries who had played their part in bringing these pressures.
But they did not discard the Christian religion as such. Christianity as practised independently of the missionaries was upheld
as the religion that would now truly be able to reintegrate society
(Lonsdale 1964: 245; Muga 1975; Peel 1968: 1).

Audrey Wipper interprets independent Churches in the same
way as Lonsdale, as protest movements among people unable to
turn the changes in society into benefits for themselves. Insecure
about their role in society, they withdrew from the world of
action. Protest movements, according to her, could take different
forms, depending on the backgrounds of the persons involved.
Sociologically, she sees independent Churches in basically the
same light as the cult of Mumbo among the Gusii at the beginning
of the century. Their only difference is that the cult of Mumbo's
beliefs came mainly from traditional religion, whereas the independent Churches turned to Christianity because the people
involved in them had been strongly influenced by Christian

missionaries. Irrespective of what form a protest movement takes, it is in its essence an attempt to explain defeat and to assure people of eventual victory. In independent Churches this is done through the belief in the imminent coming of the millennium, God's golden age of peace where all the difficulties of the present world will have been overcome (Wipper 1970: 377 and 1974).

In his study of cargo cults in Melanesia, Worsley notes the same withdrawal from the world of strains and refuge in a belief in the imminent end of the world with the arrival of the age of peace and prosperity, when all the suffering of this earth will have come to an end. But many movements have had to modify this belief over the years. He says, 'Those cults that have persisted ... have done so by severely converting chiliastic immediacy into forms of remote, "ultimate", and usually other-worldly millenarism which cannot be easily falsified.' When people found that the end of the world did not come when they expected it, they had to reinterpret their belief in the millennium. They still believed it would come, but their expectation of its immediate arrival was changed into a belief that it would come in the distant future. In most cases it was no longer seen as a radical change of the world, but as a completely new era that would come to destroy the present world with all its evils (Worsley 1968: xix).

Worsley also points out the connection between this belief in the millennium and the expression of religious sentiments through spirit possession. Social tensions cause people to isolate themselves from the world and to hope for a better life in the golden age to come. They also induce them to actions of 'motor behaviour', such as twitching or convulsions, which are interpreted as manifestations of spirit possession. He believes that this kind of action brings relief from the strains in society and a feeling of personal purity. Withdrawal from the world and spirit possession are, according to him, related phenomena, in that both are attempts to cope with social tensions. Both phenomena will therefore often be found within one religious group (Worsley 1968: 248).

The Holy Spirit movement started during a period of radical social change. The people who became involved in it had been under the influence of Christian missionaries for a number of years. They had come to accept Christianity. They had also experienced the negative aspects of associating with a mission: the paternalistic attitude of the missionaries, which gave little freedom to the converts to take an active part in worship and in church administration They had come to regard the missionaries as part of the colonial establishment. Therefore, when the outpouring of the Holy Spirit started, they eagerly grasped the opportunity this afforded for independence from the missionaries. This was at the same time seen by the Holy Spirit people themselves as independence from the colonialists. Looking in retrospect at what happened in those days, Eliakim Keverenge Atonya, the present bishop of the Lyahuka Church of East Africa, said in an interview on 27 June 1975, 'We fought for Kenya's freedom — we fought for spiritual freedom. We were praying that Lyahuka Church, or the Holy Spirit Church, should stand, and also that Kenya should have independence and that Europeans should go.'

This newly-won independence had to be asserted. And in the development of the Holy Spirit movement, the elements mentioned above as characteristic of many protest movements can be observed: isolation from the world, spirit possession, belief in the impending end of the present era, as well as the modification of this belief after some years into the expectation of an otherworldly millennium.

What Worsley calls 'motor behaviour' is the phenomenon seen in the Holy Spirit movement as possession by the Holy Spirit. When seized by the Spirit, these people were able to experience direct communication with God and a feeling of personal purity. This new experience was so forceful that they could dispense with the missionary's guidance and authority. The only thing that mattered was the continuation of their state of possession by the Holy Spirit.

When they were confronted with the choice between being members of the Friends Africa Mission or continuing with the Holy Spirit movement, many therefore chose the latter. As mentioned above, some of them later joined the Pentecostal Church where they were free to express their possession by the Holy Spirit through bodily behaviour and speaking in tongues. Others joined the Salvation Army, which also afforded a feeling of freedom and self-worth through its processions, in which every member was activated, and through its uniforms, which gave them a distinct identity.

The 'strong' supporters of the Holy Spirit movement soon gave up any affiliation with mission Churches. Persecution and expulsion from the Friends Church forced them into isolation. Rather than give up what they believed to be the true worship of God, they preferred to withdraw from their former connection with the missionaries. But their withdrawal was not only from the mission Church. They isolated themselves as much as possible from society and refused to have anything to do with other people. They believed that the end of the world was very near and that the kingdom of God was about to come. All that was important therefore was to pray and to experience the presence of God through possession by the Holy Spirit, so that they might be ready to enter the kingdom when Jesus came (interviews with Kefa Ayub Mavuru, 24 January 1975, and Japhet Zale Ambula, 2 May 1975).

Development of Specific Characteristics

The Bukoyani group of Holy Spirit people had a period of complete isolation from the world after they left the Pentecostal Church in December 1932. From January 1933 until December 1935 they only concentrated on praying and receiving the Holy Spirit. Their leaders at this time were Jacob Buluku and Daniel Sande. Daniel was regarded as a prophet. He was able to see the sins of others, and 'God could show him a lot of things' (interviews with Kefa Ayub Mavuru, 24 January 1975, and Japhet Zale Ambula, 2 May 1975). Because of this gift he came to play an important role in the development of the special characteristics of the Holy Spirit people. Jacob and Daniel guided their people to build a Church, and here they could concentrate on their worship. In an interview (1 June 1975) Japhet Zale Ambula describes the mood of those days in these words: 'They were not tired at all. Something good had entered. You did not think of eating. You just wanted to sing. You just wanted to pray. When you were standing, reading the Bible, you did not want anybody else to stand and read. You wanted just to continue and continue and continue.' They believed that the world would soon come to an end, and therefore they could not think of earthly things, 'their hearts were only in heaven.' They did not even want to dig their fields. They did not think of washing their clothes or even themselves. They only thought of praying.

In other areas the same thing happened. The Holy Spirit people went into isolation and only wanted to pray. During this time they were still being persecuted by members of the Friends Africa Mission. Perhaps the Friends still regarded them as their members, who had only been temporarily expelled as a disciplinary measure, and wanted to force them to come back (Salvation Army 1931). But other factors also contributed to the continued beatings. The attitude of the Holy Spirit people towards others, including the Friends, was one of contempt. Those who had repented all their sins and had received the baptism with the Holy Spirit had been completely cleansed. They looked upon other people as sinners, and they wanted to have nothing to do with these 'people of Satan' (interview with Jotham Eshera and Nathan Amiani, 12 April 1975). They could not eat with other people for fear of being contaminated with their sins, nor could they greet them (interview with Japhet Zale Ambula, 2 May 1975).

The Friends followed the Holy Spirit people wherever they went. Even when people were praying in private homes, they came to beat them and to disturb their meetings. This continued until around 1936. All this time the Holy Spirit people were praying for reconciliation with the Friends and an end to the persecutions. Those in Maragoli made it a practice to meet once a month for such prayers. From 1932, the Holy Spirit people from north and south Maragoli met on the 18th of every month at a place near Mbale to pray for peace and reconciliation (interviews with Eliakim Keverenge Atonya, 28 December 1974, and Japhet Zale Ambula, 19 December 1974). When the Friends eventually stopped their beatings, the Bukoyani group decided to continue to meet on the 18th of every month. In a speech during a church service at the Bukoyani headquarters of the Holy Spirit Church of East Africa on 18 January 1975, Japhet Zale Ambula said:

> When it was like that, God chose that day on which we prayed to overcome, to make it a memorial day, so that it is the day which could be looked upon. And that is the day of the 18th. And therefore, the purpose of it is this: every 18th from January until December everybody knows that we are in here.

The Bukoyani group, which is now the Holy Spirit Church of East Africa, always holds its monthly meeting on the 18th of the month. Similarly, the African Church of Holy Spirit has its specific day for monthly meetings. In this Church it is the 20th of the month, and this date was revealed to the people in Isukha and Idakho through a prophecy around 1930 (interview with Timotheo Hezekiah Shitsimi, 6 June 1976).

Many customs now characteristic of the Holy Spirit Churches originated in the years of isolation. As already mentioned, they did not want to greet other people for fear of being contaminated with their sins. When the persecution by Friends decreased around 1956, they relaxed this attitude, though only to the extent that they could now greet by clapping their hands. They still did not want to shake hands with other people. This rule is still upheld by most members of the Holy Spirit Church of East Africa. But people in the other Holy Spirit Churches now shake hands like everybody else (interview with Japhet Zale Ambula, 2 May 1975).

The rule about not eating with others, even with relatives, persisted for a long time. But around 1940 some began to mix more freely with non-members, and gradually this custom has disappeared (interview with Jotham Eshera, 12 April 1975).

As a result of their belief that the world would soon come to an end, the Holy Spirit people did not want to send their children to school. If the world was not going to continue, there was no need for education, only for prayer. Also, most of the schools in the area belonged to the Friends Africa Mission, and it would probably have been difficult for the Holy Spirit people to get their children accepted in those schools, had they wanted to try. This negative attitude to education persisted for a long time among the majority of the Holy Spirit people. Nowadays many send their children to school. But the attitude of the early days is reflected in the relatively low level of education among members of the Holy Spirit Churches (interview with Eliakim Keverenge Atonya, 27 June 1975).

Another important feature of these early days was the complete rejection of all kinds of medicine. They believed that diseases were caused by demons, so to go to a traditional healer to have him cast out the demons would have been equivalent to 'worshipping other gods' and would therefore have been completely against the Christian faith. Seeking treatment from a hospital would also show a lack of faith. The Holy Spirit people believed in the supreme power of God in all areas of life, and the demons that caused disease therefore had to be chased out through prayer and faith in

God alone. This attitude still persists. Though many members of the Holy Spirit Churches now go to a hospital if they become ill, it is still regarded as evidence of weakness in faith (interview with Timotheo Hezekiah Shitsimi, 6 June 1976).

Many other practices dating back to the days of isolation are still upheld. These include the use of 'symbols' such as special clothes and beards, which serve as marks of identification for the Holy Spirit people and thereby set them apart from other members of society. They found in Revelation 6:9–11 that those who had suffered for the sake of the word of God were given white robes:

> When he opened the fifth seal, I saw under the altar the souls of those who had been slain for the word of God and for the witness they had borne; they cried out with a loud voice, 'O Sovereign Lord, holy and true, how long before thou wilt judge and avenge our blood on those who dwell upon the earth?' Then they were each given a white robe and told to rest a little longer, until the number of their fellow servants and their brethren should be complete, who were to be killed as they themselves had been.

And they believed that God had in the same way directed them to wear long white garments as a sign of purity.

The use of turbans by the men is a pattern learnt from pictures of Jesus and His disciples. Eliakim Keverenge Atonya pointed out a scriptural basis for this practice in that John 20:6–7 shows that Jesus had a piece of cloth on his head when he was buried: 'Then Simon Peter came, following him, and went into the tomb; he saw the linen cloths lying, and the napkin, which had been on his head, not lying with the linen cloths but rolled up in a place by itself.'

Another characteristic of the Holy Spirit people is that they always wear a red cross on their clothes. This symbol seems to have come into use as early as 1927, and the only explanation given for it is that the Holy Spirit directed them to wear it. There are nowadays slight differences in the crosses which serve to distinguish the members of one Holy Spirit Church from those of another. The Holy Spirit Church of East Africa has a big cross, which often covers the whole chest; the African Church of Holy Spirit has a smaller cross, while the Lyahuka Church of East Africa has a circle around its cross.

During the years of isolation they also found that they were told by God that the men should let their beards grow. Originally they did not want to wear beards, but whenever they tried to shave they would cut themselves. Though this may have been due to physical exhaustion from praying and receiving the Spirit, the Holy Spirit people interpreted it as a command from God that they should no longer shave their beards. Also, some members still have very long hair. During those first years when they thought only of praying, they did not care about personal hygiene. They were too occupied with the Holy Spirit to bother about washing or cutting their hair. It became a rule that they should not cut their hair. Nowadays only a minority of the members uphold this custom (interviews with Japhet Zale Ambula, 2 May 1975, and Eliakim Keverenge Atonya, 27 June 1975).

By the middle of the 1930s, a pattern of symbols and behaviour had therefore begun to emerge which served to keep the Holy Spirit people together and to give them a distinct identity in the eyes of other people. They had not yet formed an organized Church, but had developed enough characteristics in common to feel a considerably strengthened sense of belonging to one group as distinct from other Churches.

Government Reaction to the Holy Spirit Movement

In the mid-1930s, the Holy Spirit people were still too busy praying in the Spirit in expectation of the impending end of the world to give much thought to forming a Church organization. This lack of interest in establishing a Church was reflected in the absence of an official name for the movement. Members of the Friends Africa Mission would normally call them *avahuji* or *Lyahuka*, and those of them who were in Isukha were also often referred to as *avakambuli*.[6] They themselves would normally use the name *Avandu va Roho*, and many outsiders would call them by the same name, but in Kiswahili, *Dini ya Roho* (interviews with Nathan Amiani, 12 April 1975, Japhet Zale Ambula, 13 January 1975, and Kefa Ayub Mavuru, 24 January 1975).[7]

6. *Avahuji* means 'people who have broken away', *Lyahuka* 'a group that has broken away' and *avakambuli* 'those who say what they have to [confess] openly'.
7. *Avandu va Roho* means 'People of the Spirit', and *Dini ya Roho* 'Religion of the Spirit'.

In 1934 another group called Dini ya Roho was set up among the Luo in Wanga location. These people had been members of the Anglican Church and had for years had a strained relationship with their Wanga neighbours. When a revival started among the Luo in 1933, feelings of religious superiority exacerbated the already tense situation. In January 1934 matters came to a head when two Wanga men were killed by the Luo. The Wanga retaliated by setting fire to a number of houses belonging to the Luo and several people were burnt to death, including the Revd Alphayo Odongo, who had been a pastor in the Anglican Church. When he had given his support to the revival, his relationship with his Anglican superiors had become bad. His death now caused his supporters to make the break with the Anglican Church final, and they formed the Dini ya Roho (Greschat 1969: 265).

These riots made the government officers very conscious of the political dangers inherent in Dini ya Roho. They believed that the Dini ya Roho among the Abaluyia people was identical to the one among the Luo in Wanga (North Kavirondo District 1938a; Native Intelligence 1940). As a matter of fact, there was some connection between the two groups. Lonsdale (1964: 359) mentions that the Anglican evangelist who brought the revival to the Luo in the first place had been influenced by the Holy Spirit movement in Maragoli and, after the riots in Wanga and the establishment of Dini ya Roho there, some of the Luo members had decided to seek contact with the Holy Spirit people in south Maragoli. At Daniel Sande's funeral, in 1936, the Maragoli people suddenly saw five strangers approach who, like themselves, were wearing crosses on their clothes. The Maragolians had apparently not at that time known about the existence of the other group. They were now told about what had happened two years earlier. Some of them accompanied the Luo when they went home, to see the graves of those who had been killed. The two groups continued to have some fellowship with each other for a number of years (interview with Japhet Zale Ambula, 13 January 1975).

Not all the Holy Spirit people among the Abaluyia became involved with the Dini ya Roho in Wanga. The government officers, however, believed that it was one movement, for they observed some of the same characteristics among the Holy Spirit people as they had seen in Dini ya Roho. The feeling of religious superiority which had led to riots there was evident here too.

People who had received the Holy Spirit and believed themselves to be cleansed of all sin were refusing to eat or speak with others, even with their relatives. They regarded other people as sinners, as people of Satan, and in their preaching and behaviour they showed them that they felt superior. From the government's point of view this attitude was potentially dangerous, so a close watch was kept on the Holy Spirit people.

By around 1936 the members of the Friends Africa Mission had all but stopped beating the Holy Spirit people. They had probably realized that the persecution was not going to bring them back to the Friends Church. Now a different kind of persecution started, this time by the government. In 1936 Eliakim Keverenge Atonya was imprisoned for erecting a church building illegally (interview with Eliakim Keverenge Atonya, 3 January 1975). In the same year the three leading figures at Endeli, Enis Kadali, Daudi Sagida and Joseph Chegero, were all imprisoned 'because of their way of preaching' (interview with Elfas Ojiango Sagida, 1 March 1975). The imprisonment did not last long, but it was a warning that the government was becoming increasingly concerned about the behaviour of the Holy Spirit people.

One reason why the government officers felt uneasy about this movement was that it had no recognized leader who could be held responsible for the actions of the people. As Kefa Ayub Mavuru (interview, 24 January 1975) said, 'At the beginning there were no leaders. There were different groups in different villages, but they wanted no leader. They wanted the Holy Spirit to lead them. And this lack of leaders was one reason why government persecuted them.' To be sure, there were certain personalities who had gradually come to be looked upon by the others as their leaders, including Daniel Sande and Jacob Buluku in south Maragoli, Joseph Chegero and Daudi Sagida in north Maragoli, Samson Libeya in Isukha, and Julius Mung'asia in Idakho (Keverenge et al. n.d.). But these were all unofficial local leaders; there was no overall leader of the whole Holy Spirit movement

In 1939 the district commissioner called a meeting with some of the more prominent members of the Holy Spirit movement. Shortly before there had been difficulties at Keverenge Atonya's home, when he had again built a church illegally and had been forced to pull it down. Also, many people had been staying at his place for weeks, including a number of women. This had made the

Holy Spirit people very unpopular among the relatives of these women, as there was a belief that they practised 'free love' (North Kavirondo District 1938b).

The district commissioner now called this meeting in the hope that the Holy Spirit people would bend under some kind of authority that could be answerable to the government. Pentecostal missionaries had also been invited to the meeting, and they tried to persuade the Holy Spirit people to join them. But their offer was completely rejected.

The district commissioner then asked who among them was the overall leader, and he got different answers. Samson Libeya claimed that he was the leader. Isaiah Maleya, who together with Japhet Zale Ambula had taken over the leadership of the south Maragoli group after the deaths of Jacob Buluku and Daniel Sande, said, according to Kefa Ayub Mavuru, 'DC! This meeting started at our place, and the leader must be there.' Everyone regarded their own area as the most important, and the leader there was therefore seen as the overall leader. When the district commissioner eventually asked Kefa Ayub Mavuru, he answered, 'We do not have leaders, only chiefs. The church of God should not choose its leaders in court.' The district commissioner now realized that the meeting would not result in any leader being recognized by everybody. In his own words, 'They could not agree as to which of them was the leader, they could not control their people, they seemed well meaning, but hopeless.'

After a warning that they had to use all their influence to discourage the 'objectionable practices' of their members, the Holy Spirit people were allowed to leave the meeting (North Kavirondo District 1939; interview with Kefa Ayub Mavuru, 10 June 1975).

When they had been called to this meeting, they had thought that the government was going to take serious measures against them. Kefa Ayub Mavuru said that they in fact thought that they were going to be killed. When this did not happen, they went from the meeting singing with joy. However, the district commissioner's purpose in calling the meeting had not been fulfilled. There was still no recognized leader of the Holy Spirit people whom the government could hold responsible for what happened within the movement and the suspicion against them continued. An intelligence report about them in 1940 stated that the Revd Alphayo Odongo had been one of the leaders of the 'Holy Rollers' as it called them.[8] It goes on to describe what outsiders regarded as the main characteristics of these people: 'Among their beliefs is Faith-healing to the extent that they will not remove a jigger from a foot; Free Love; Refusal to shave and refusal to submit to any discipline.'

The matter of discipline was what worried the administrators most; and the report shows that they were aware of the passive resistance to the government inherent in the movement. It continues: 'The sect is Anti-European and Anti-Government insomuch as it does not believe in discipline and appears to be ruled entirely by religious ecstasy.' Although there was no immediate cause for concern, since the movement was not at that time 'abnormally active', the report warns that, 'The body must be considered potentially dangerous, as in the hands of a clever agent, it might be a serious embarrassment to the local Administration' (Native Intelligence 1940). When this report was written, the Holy Spirit people were already slowly beginning to adjust themselves to the wishes of the government. In 1940 the Bukoyani group decided to form a Church of its own, independent of the rest of the movement. The reason given for this is that on 6 January 1940 they were told by the Holy Spirit that they should no longer worship on Sundays. The proper day to rest and to hold church services was Saturday. When the other Holy Spirit people refused to follow the Bukoyani group in changing the day of worship to Saturday, the people in south Maragoli decided to break away from the fellowship and to set up a Church of their own. The original leaders in this area had died, Daniel Sande in 1936 and Jacob Buluku in 1938. Japhet Zale Ambula and Isaiah Maleya, who had been strong supporters of the movement from the beginning, had taken over as leaders. Therefore, when the new Church was formed they were ready to assume its leadership (interview with Japhet Zale Ambula, 13 January 1975).

This development is not seen by the Holy Spirit people as an adjustment to the government's demands, but it did reflect the Bukoyani group's growing wish for recognition by the administration and for the peace that would follow such recognition. The

8. Other names used in the report are *Watu wa Roho*, 'People of the Spirit' in Kiswahili, *Joroho*, the same name in Dholuo, and *Wakambuli*.

other branches of the Holy Spirit movement were not yet willing to bend under one leader who could be answerable to the government, but the people in south Maragoli gathered around these two people, whom they considered the true leaders, and formed their Church irrespective of the opinion of the others.

When the south Maragoli group decided to set up its own Church in 1940, the Holy Spirit people in north Maragoli, Isukha and Idakho had not yet agreed to any overall leader, but they were slowly beginning to adapt to the society around them. At around the time of the split between north and south, the people in north Maragoli were giving up their strict isolation. They were becoming increasingly conscious of the status of their group in the eyes of others. When it became apparent that the end of the world was not as near at hand as they had thought, life with other people began to resume its importance. They developed a wish for their group to be recognized as a Church and to enjoy the same status as the mission Churches. And around 1940 they began to put up church buildings near to the roads, 'in order to show people that we were now like any other Church'.

Their home life was also affected by this change of attitude. They realized that they could only develop peaceful relations with other people and become accepted by them if they gave up treating them as less pure than themselves. Jotham Eshera says that what made them change was 1. Corinthians 13, especially v.l: 'If I speak in the tongues of men and of angels, but have not love, I am a noisy gong or a clanging cymbal.' When they had read this verse, they thought, 'You are a Christian, I am a Christian, so why? When you do not even drink?' These people had changed from their former belief that only they were pure and would be saved, which was closely bound up with their expectation that the world would soon come to an end. As this expectation faded, they had to accommodate to the society around them and this made them realize that others might be as true in their Christianity as they were. The immediate result was that from 1939 members of the Holy Spirit movement in north Maragoli began to eat with other people (interview with Jotham Eshera, 12 April 1975).

This gradual opening up by the Holy Spirit people towards the world around them once more became apparent in 1946 when the government again asked them to find a leader who could be answerable for all of them to the government. This time their wish to be recognized as a Church led them to agree, and Solomon Ahindukha from Isukha was chosen to be this leader. The main reason why the choice fell on him was that he had more education than other leaders at that time. He was able to speak Kiswahili, and he was working as a cook for Europeans, which, in the eyes of the Holy Spirit people, gave him special abilities to talk with them. The balance between the Isukha–Idakho group and the north Maragoli group was kept when Shem Ajega from north Maragoli was chosen as Solomon's deputy (interview with Kefa Ayub Mavuru, 24 January 1975; Keverenge et al. n.d.). Here again, education played a role. The original leaders in north Maragoli, Joseph Chegero and Daudi Sagida, had very little or no education and could therefore not be accepted by government officers to represent the group (interviews with Petro Sida and Zebedaioh Malolo, 14 June 1975, and Japhet Zale Ambula, 16 June 1975).

This change of attitude among the Holy Spirit people from around 1940, with their gradual bending to the government's demands and their opening up towards other people, was the decisive step towards the formation of respectable Churches that would be on a par with other Churches. Originally, these people had been forced to isolate themselves. The religious practices they believed to be right, and which they were not prepared to give up, had met with opposition from other people. They had been persecuted, first by the Friends and later by the government. The persecution had been added to the difficulties that had in the first place made them so readily accept the purifying experience of receiving the Holy Spirit. This experience, coupled with their belief in the imminent end of the world, had made them abandon normal life and isolate themselves in prayer. As time passed, their expectation that the world would come to an end had faded and they were forced to recognize that the millennium might be further off than they had at first thought. They now faced the challenge of finding a way of living in the present world without giving up their essential beliefs and characteristics. This was what made them begin slowly to turn away from their former hostile attitude towards all outsiders. And as they began to adjust themselves to society, the persecutions stopped. This in turn gave them the opportunity to relax their isolation and to begin to organize their movement openly along the lines they believed the Holy Spirit had shown them.

Consolidation and Growth

The Southern Group of Holy Spirit People
After 1940, when the Holy Spirit people around Bukoyani decided to present their own leaders to the government and thereby assert their independence of those further north, there was very little contact between the two groups. From then onwards they developed separately, although along parallel lines. The similarities in their histories can be accounted for by their common origin in the Friends Africa Mission, by their similar cultural backgrounds, in that the members of both groups belonged to Abaluyia tribes, and by the modern social setting which was very much alike in north and south.

The Bukoyani group had become formally established as a Church in 1940. But it was not yet registered as a legal society under government law, and its freedom to preach in other parts of the country was therefore to some extent limited. Also, the isolationism of its founding years was still an important feature of the Church. Adjusting to the society around them was a gradual process and it appears that there were only few attempts at expansion during the first decade after 1940.

In 1952, on the initiative of the administrative officers, the Church was registered as a legal body under the Societies Act (interview with Japhet Zale Ambula, 13 January 1975). This was a time of tension in the country as a whole. From 1944 the Dini ya Msambwa movement among the Bukusu, with its ardent anti-European and anti-government attitude, had created problems for the administration (Kenya Government 1950; Wipper 1971: 157–91). The administrative officers feared that the latent anti-government sentiments in other *dini*s would change into the same kind of open resistance. Every year from 1949 until 1952, the district commissioner mentions these other religious bodies in his annual reports. He finds that they have given no trouble, but this is not enough to assure him that they constitute no danger: 'These breakaway sects from established (usually Protestant) Missions are always somewhat of a worry since their danger or relative harmlessness usually depends on the degree of crankiness of the leaders' (North Nyanza District 1952). But tensions were not only to be found in the western part of the country. In 1952 the Mau Mau revolt against the colonial government started in Central Province, and the state of emergency that followed this uprising lasted until 1960 (Rosberg and Nottingham 1966). During the 1950s the colonial government was therefore concerned about any movement that might be considered a potential danger to the stability of the country. And this was the reason why the Church that had been formed by the Holy Spirit people in south Maragoli was asked to register under government rules and to hand in a constitution to the government.

The people themselves would have preferred to have called their Church Dini ya Roho. But the officer in charge of the registration told them that they had to register under a name that would be understandable to the British, and it was he who decided that the name of the Church was to be the direct translation into English of *Dini ya Roho*: Holy Spirit Church (interview with Japhet Zale Ambula, 13 January 1975).

Once the Church had been registered as a legal society it had freedom to expand into new areas. A number of people from south Maragoli had gone to Nairobi to work there, and they had brought their religion with them. The same thing happened during the 1950s when some of the members of the Holy Spirit Church migrated to northern Tanzania and Uganda: wherever they settled they established branches of their Church. In 1957 (according to Barrett et al. 1973: 186) the government asked the Holy Spirit Church to re-register and to write a more detailed constitution. Because it had spread to new areas since the time of the first registration, even outside Kenya, the Church decided to make an addition to its name, and it now became the Holy Spirit Church of East Africa (interview with Japhet Zale Ambula, 13 January 1975).

The growth of this Church continued after 1957, though it did not spread to many new areas. At present it has eight main centres for its activities, concentrated in the southern part of Kakamega District, in and around Nairobi, and in south Nyanza. The precise number of members is not known. A register of members exists, but the leaders admit that this register is not up to date 'because of a lack of education' (interview with Japhet Zale Ambula and Christopher Ondolo, 27 January 1975). The *Kenya Churches Handbook* gives the number of the total Christian community of this Church as 3000 and the number of adult members as 660 (Barrett et al. 1973: 186). But judging from attendances at the

18th meetings at the Bukoyani church, where between 500 and 600 people can be gathered, these figures are probably lower than the actual number of members.

As the membership of the Holy Spirit Church of East Africa grew, the need arose for a more fixed pattern of organization. From the beginning these people had met in small groups in their villages, and the village congregations with the close fellowship that is only possible in such small communities is still the most important organizational level in this Church (interview with Japhet Zale Ambula, 27 January 1975). As we have seen, the 18th of the month soon assumed a special importance among these people as the date on which they had prayed for peace with the members of the Friends Africa Mission. When reconciliation with the Friends was obtained, they decided that on the 18th of every month they must gather from a number of villages for a big meeting to commemorate the day that brought peace. Therefore, from around 1936 this Church worshipped at the level of both village and monthly meetings.

The pattern of having gatherings for worship at different levels is a feature of the Society of Friends. In this Church members meet weekly at their village meetings, then people from a number of villages come together once a month for a monthly meeting. Every three months there is a quarterly meeting with members coming together from a number of monthly meetings, and at the highest level is the yearly meeting at which all the other meetings are represented. Each level of meetings has its corresponding organizational set-up, so that the ranks of leadership rise from village leaders to monthly-meeting leaders, through quarterly-meeting leaders, up to the top leadership of the yearly meeting.

When the Holy Spirit Church of East Africa felt the need to create a more formal system of Church government they naturally chose the model of the Friends Africa Mission, for this was the mission Church with which they had had the closest contact. But the Church was not suddenly organized along these lines. There was a gradual growth in the awareness of the need for a more formal administration of Church affairs. Japhet Zale Ambula said in an interview (27 January 1975) that 'After we came out of the Friends Church we were persecuted, we were outcasts, and only recently did we begin to recover from this psychologically. Therefore we are only now thinking of streamlining the Church.'

Because the Holy Spirit people did not, at the time of the persecutions, want to associate with things of this world — they only wanted the experience of being filled with the Holy Spirit — they had no thought of organizing their fellowship into any specific pattern.

Only after the Church had been registered and had spread to new areas did the need for a fixed pattern of church administration arise. In 1966 it was decided at some of the monthly meetings to form a quarterly meeting, and now this higher level of organization has been introduced in all parts of the Church. But this decision grew from the needs of the individual monthly meetings and was not imposed by the top leadership of the Church (interview with Christopher Ondolo, 27 January 1975). The yearly-meeting level, to use the terminology of the Friends, has been there from the beginning in that throughout the history of the Church the leaders at Bukoyani have been regarded as the core that keeps the Church together. At the beginning, Bukoyani was the village where the Holy Spirit movement was centred. But as the Church grew, it has remained the centre and is now the headquarters of the whole Church.

Just as the pattern of organizational levels has been taken over from the Friends Africa Mission, so has the pattern of leadership positions. The Friends have at each level a presiding clerk, a recording clerk, a treasurer and their deputies. The Holy Spirit Church of East Africa follows the same pattern, though here again it can be seen that this Church has not laid much emphasis on a formal structure. At headquarters this pattern is adhered to, but at other levels the leadership system is looser. Christopher Ondolo sees this as a weakness, which he attributes to a lack of education among the Church's top leaders. He hopes that as a new generation of more educated members grows up, the organization of the Church will come to follow a stricter pattern, so that they will 'find out who leads what section of the Church' (interview with Christopher Ondolo, 27 January 1975).

Although organization has not been accorded much importance until recently, the top leaders at Bukoyani appear to have full control of the Church. The archbishop, Japhet Zale Ambula, and his deputy, Bishop Isaiah Maleya, command considerable respect from members because they were among the founders of the Holy Spirit movement and suffered beatings during the first difficult years. Though their titles may be influenced by the Church Missionary Society station at nearby Maseno, they also reflect an important difference from the leadership among Friends. That Church is basically democratic in that each local congregation can make its voice heard at the various organizational levels, even up to the yearly meeting. But in the Holy Spirit Church of East Africa it appears that the archbishop, together with his committee of top leaders, makes most of the important decisions in the Church. While he cannot possibly be described as a dictator, for receiving the Holy Spirit is basically an individual experience and renders importance to each member of the Church, the archbishop is the man who is expected to guide the Church in all ways. He is the religious head and, together with a few elderly people including a couple of prophetesses, is in charge of spreading the true teachings of the Church to all its members (interview with Japhet Zale Ambula and Christopher Ondolo, 27 January 1975). He is also the arbitrator when difficulties arise among members, for they are not allowed to take each other to court (interview with Japhet Zale Ambula, 13 January 1975). Finally, he is the main link between his Church and the government.

These duties of the archbishop correspond rather closely with those of clan heads before the introduction of a colonial administration completely changed their role. Wagner (1949: 77) points out that the office of a clan head combined three functions: that of a judge, that of a priest and that of a political leader. However, the same man would not necessarily perform all these functions. He would often share his duties with a council of clan elders. The same pattern can be observed in the Holy Spirit Church of East Africa, in that the archbishop often shares with his committee his functions as arbitrator, religious leader and the 'politician' who has to make things run smoothly within the Church and in its relations with the government.

Describing African independent Churches in South Africa, Sundkler (1970: 100) points to the parallel between leaders of 'Ethiopian' Churches and the traditional chiefs on the one hand, and leaders of 'Zionist' Churches and the prophets in traditional society on the other. However, the Holy Spirit Church of East Africa does not fit Sundkler's distinction between 'Ethiopian'- and 'Zionist'-type Churches. In the Holy Spirit Church of East Africa prophecy and faith healing are important phenomena, as they are in 'Zionist' Churches, but at the same time many of the mission Church's characteristics have also been taken over, as they have in the 'Ethiopian' Churches. Nevertheless, Sundkler's observation that the leadership of independent Churches reflects the pattern in traditional society does apply to the Holy Spirit Church of East Africa.

Since its split from the rest of the Holy Spirit movement in 1940, the Holy Spirit Church of East Africa has gone through many changes. Its registration, though forced by the government, helped break down its isolationist attitude towards the outside world. In the 1950s and 1960s it spread to new areas of Kenya and into Uganda and Tanzania. Its increased membership caused it to develop a more structured system of organization, with top-level leadership positions corresponding to those of the Friends. However, the functions performed by these top leaders, and especially by the archbishop, conform to those performed by the traditional clan leadership. The Holy Spirit Church of East Africa has thereby created a pattern of leadership that combines the pre-colonial authority system, which included both secular and religious matters, with Church leadership as known in the mission Churches. This combination, which has developed naturally, has helped foster that reintegration of society the mission Churches had failed to bring about.

The Northern Group of Holy Spirit People
In 1946 the Holy Spirit people in Isukha, Idakho and north Maragoli bent to government pressure and elected Solomon Ahindukha and Shem Ajega as their official leaders. They had come to realize the advantages of a good relationship with the administration and of the respectability in the eyes of others that would follow upon such recognition. But there were not yet any attempts to structure the loosely connected congregations of Holy Spirit people into a more fixed pattern of organization. Solomon Ahindukha was simply these people's spokesman before the government officers. But he made no attempt to assume power over the internal affairs of the people (interview with Kefa Ayub Mavuru, 10 June 1975). Firmer leadership and attempts to organize the movement did not start until after his death.

Solomon died in 1952 and Kefa Ayub Mavuru was elected as his successor. At that time Mavuru was the most highly educated person in the Holy Spirit movement, and his membership of a chiefly lineage, in that he was a son of the former chief of Isukha, Ichivini, made him the obvious choice for the leadership, at least in the eyes of the people from Isukha and Idakho (interviews with Petro Sida and Zebedaioh Malolo, 14 June 1975, and Jeremiah Murila, 26 June 1975). He was soon to prove a strong leader. His prophetic gifts (interview with Peter Ihaji, 25 June 1975) and charismatic personality made him able to gather the support of the Holy Spirit people in his moves to consolidate and extend the work of the movement.

Kefa Ayub Mavuru has combined his prophetic gift with a style of leadership which fits into the pattern of the chiefly lineage from which he comes. As is the case with Japhet Zale Ambula in the Holy Spirit Church of East Africa, his functions in the Church correspond closely with those of a traditional clan head. He is at one and the same time the religious head of his Church, the arbitrator in disputes, and the politically minded person who tries to keep the balance between the various sections of the Church and who represents the Church to the outside world. Like Zale Ambula, he has a committee of elders who help him run the affairs of the Church, but the final decision in all matters is his (interview with Peter Ihaji, 25 June 1975).

Soon after his assumption of the leadership of the Holy Spirit people, Kefa Ayub Mavuru displayed features that were characteristic of two kinds of leaders in the traditional background of his followers: those of a dream prophet and those of a clan head. He incorporated religious and social leadership in one person, and was thus able to lead his followers in all aspects of their lives. The reason why he became such a strong leader from the very beginning is probably that the members of the Holy Spirit movement saw in him the person who would be able to restore the unity of sacred and secular, which had been so seriously disrupted by the coming of the colonial administration and the changes that had taken place since then.

Under his leadership the Holy Spirit movement soon spread to new areas. Members who worked away from home preached their message at the places to which they went, and this resulted in new congregations being founded in those areas. Many had gone to Nairobi, and from there the Holy Spirit movement spread to Meru and Embu through people who returned home from work. A number of people, especially from Maragoli, migrated to south Nyanza because of the pressure on land in their home area. Some went to northern Tanzania, and some to Uganda. In all these places they formed branches of their Church and won a number of the local people over to their movement (interview with Kefa Ayub Mavuru, 24 January 1975).

Wherever the movement spread, Mavuru ensured that it became properly organized as part of his Church. He would often travel to the respective places and officially open the new meetings himself. It was when he was about to travel to Kisii in 1955 to open the branch there that his movement got its official name. Until then they had used the original names, Avandu va Roho or Dini ya Roho. Now that the Church was spreading the government wanted it to have an official name, and before he set out Mavuru was called by the Special Branch and given a rubber stamp for use by his Church. He had not been consulted as to which name he would prefer. The Special Branch officer simply presented him with the stamp which gave the name of the Church as 'African Church of Holy Spirit' and his own title as 'High Priest'. Although nobody in the Church had had any say in the choice of the name or their leader's title, the Special Branch decision was fully accepted. The Special Branch was also involved when Meru and Embu became official branches of the Church in 1960. Mavuru sees this interference from the government as a help, for it enabled him to organize his Church along fixed lines (interview with Kefa Ayub Mavuru, 24 January 1975).

In 1957 the administrative officers insisted that the African Church of Holy Spirit be officially registered under the Societies Act. The activities of Mau Mau and of Dini ya Msambwa during that time made the government very suspicious of any unregistered group, so the Church was faced with the choice between being proscribed or being registered. It chose registration (interview with Kefa Ayub Mavuru, 10 June 1975).

Registration made the African Church of Holy Spirit appear more respectable to other people, and this resulted in a growth in the number of members. Not only did the Church spread to new territories, but the membership also increased substantially in its original home area. When being a member of this Church no longer carried any danger of government persecution, many joined it, and as the number of members increased, the organization was strengthened. The pattern of organization in the African Church of Holy Spirit parallels that of the Friends Church, with its village, monthly, quarterly and yearly meeting levels, and with a chairman, secretary and treasurer at each level. There are a number of other leadership positions besides these, but the pattern of the Friends Africa Mission is clearly discernible (interview with Peter Ihaji, 25 June 1975).

In the early 1960s Mavuru began to organize the Church along these lines, and he made the north Maragoli group into a quarterly meeting under the leadership of Eliakim Keverenge Atonya. The Church had gained adherents in south Maragoli and, here again, a quarterly meeting was opened at around the same time (interview with Kefa Ayub Mavuru, 10 June 1975). Another quarterly meeting was also opened at Kabras. Though the first member from that area joined the Church in 1938, it was not until around 1950 that it gained many adherents (interview with Timotheo Hezekiah Shitsimi, 20 February 1975). Since that time, however, the congregations in Kabras have grown very fast, and at present the African Church of Holy Spirit appears to be more active there than anywhere else.

In 1960 this Church became a member of the National Christian Council of Kenya (Mavuru and Ihaji 1975). This added to its status and since that time many people have wanted to become members. At present the African Church of Holy Spirit has six quarterly meetings in Kakamega District and four others in south Nyanza, Nairobi, Embu and Meru. It has also spread to the areas around Eldoret and Molo and, as mentioned before, to Uganda and Tanzania, though there are not enough members in each of these places to make up a quarterly meeting (interview with Peter Ihaji, 25 June 1975). As in the Holy Spirit Church of East Africa, it is difficult to establish the exact number of members. The *Kenya Churches Handbook* says that in 1973 there were 3352 adult members and a total Christian community of 5455 (Barrett et al. 1973: 184), but Church sources claim that the total number of members is nearly 20000 (Mavuru and Ihaji 1975). Judging from attendance at monthly and quarterly meetings, where there are often 200 to 300 people or more, and considering the number of monthly meetings, which must be around 45, this number is probably more accurate than the number given in the *Kenya Churches Handbook*.

By the time the Holy Spirit movement had reached the stage of bending to the government's demand for an official spokesman, a new period of growth had begun, which was accompanied by a strengthening of the Church's organizational set-up. The Holy Spirit Church of East Africa and the African Church of Holy Spirit were both registered in the 1950s, bringing higher status and more members to both, but as the Churches grew in membership, the danger arose that the top leadership would be unable to satisfy all members. From time to time sections within the Churches did express dissatisfaction with certain aspects of church life (interview with Peter Ihaji, 25 June 1975). In the 1960s and 1970s two such sections got out of hand for the African Church of Holy Spirit, which resulted in their separation and the formation of two independent Churches.

Division into Four Holy Spirit Churches

Split Between North and South
The first division of the Holy Spirit movement occurred in 1940 when the Bukoyani group decided to begin to worship on Saturdays. The rest of the movement did not want to follow them in this decision, and the Bukoyani people therefore decided to form their own Church, which would be independent of the others. They now gave the names of their leaders to the government as those who would be answerable for the actions of their members. As mentioned above, an important reason for this split was probably that the people at Bukoyani wanted to improve their relationship with the colonial administration so that they could carry on with their church work without outside interference.

Another factor may also have contributed to their decision to break off from the rest of the Holy Spirit movement — the traditional division between south Maragoli on the one hand and north Maragoli and Idakho on the other. According to tribal history, there had been a serious quarrel between two sons of Mulogoli, the ancestor of all Logoli people, during which one of them had killed the other. As a result, the sons of the deceased brother decided to migrate away from their relatives and to settle further north, thereby dividing the Maragoli area into a northern and southern part. Later on, the people in south Maragoli decided to fight against those further north. To protect themselves against

their southern relatives, the northerners entered into an alliance
with the Idakho. In pre-colonial times relations between north and
south Maragoli were therefore relatively bad (Wagner 1949: 59).

Lonsdale observes that the break in 1940 was exactly along
these traditional lines, with south Maragoli seeking independence
from the people in north Maragoli, who remained in fellowship
with those in Idakho and Isukha in the Holy Spirit movement
(Lonsdale 1964: 359). Sundkler (1970: 167) points out that tribal
issues play an important role in the secessions of one Church from
another in South Africa, and it is highly likely that the traditional
cool feelings towards north Maragoli played an unconscious role
in the split of the Bukoyani group from the rest of the Holy Spirit
movement. The example of the Dini ya Roho among the Luo in
Wanga, who worshipped on Saturdays, probably contributed to
their decision to take that day as their holy day, although they
themselves interpret it as a revelation from God. Once this theological issue had come up it provided them with the necessary
justification for forming a Church of their own.

There is today no animosity between the Holy Spirit Church of
East Africa and the rest of the Holy Spirit people. It is accepted by
everybody that the Holy Spirit commanded the Bukoyani group to
worship on Saturdays, and this is seen as a valid reason for breaking off from the others. To understand this peaceful relationship it
is probably important to recognize that when the Bukoyani group
became independent there was no organized Church in the north.
They formed a Church where before there had been only scattered
congregations. But they did not break off from an already established Church, and therefore no struggles for leadership between
different personalities took place. This is an important difference
from the later divisions where, as will be shown below, groups
already belonging to one Church, the African Church of Holy
Spirit, decided to break away from its leadership to set up their
own Churches with their own leaders. Personal rivalries were
involved in these separations, and this resulted in negative feelings
between the mother Church and the newly independent Churches.

Two Groups in One Church: The African Church of Holy Spirit
When the African Church of Holy Spirit was registered with the
government in 1957, one of the points mentioned in the constitution of the Church was that monthly meetings must be held on

the 20th of every month (Constitution n.d.). This date had been revealed to a prophet of the Church around 1930, and the people in Isukha and Idakho regarded it as an important matter that the prophecy was adhered to (interview with Timotheo Hezekiah Shitsimi, 6 June 1976). Possibly the importance attached to the date of the monthly meeting during those early years had to do with the wish of the Holy Spirit people to assert their independence from the missionaries of the Friends Africa Mission. Like the baptism with the Spirit, the use of the 20th for monthly meetings had been revealed directly to these people, and thereby the missionaries lost their importance as the bringers of the word of God. Even in later years this date has remained important as a mark of identification of the African Church of Holy Spirit. Whereas before it served the purpose of demonstrating the freedom of the Holy Spirit people from missionary guidance, it now came to mark the difference between one part of the Holy Spirit movement and another.

Not all the Holy Spirit people in the northern locations agreed to hold their monthly meetings on the 20th. It was mainly those in Isukha and Idakho who saw this date as important. Many of those in north Maragoli never changed the date of the monthly meeting, but continued to hold it on the 30th like the Friends (interviews with Eliakim Keverenge Atonya, 28 December 1974, and Petro Sida, 22 March 1975). It is interesting to note that this difference concerning dates ran along tribal lines, Isukha and Idakho adhering to one rule and north Maragoli to another. The distance between the two groups explains why different traditions were developed in the two areas. For a number of years the question of dates did not assume any importance since there were no attempts to gather the individual congregations into one Church, and therefore no attempts at forced uniformity. Later on this difference became an issue when the people from north Maragoli sought independence from the African Church of Holy Spirit.

As mentioned, when these people elected their first spokesman in 1946, the balance was kept between Isukha and Idakho on the one hand, and north Maragoli on the other, in that Solomon Ahindukha from Isukha became the leader and Shem Ajega from north Maragoli his deputy. Shem soon died and, since nobody else was elected to his post, Solomon continued as the only official leader of the group until his death in 1952 (interview with Kefa

Ayub Mavuru, 10 June 1975). When he died the question was raised of whether the next leader should be from north Maragoli, Isukha or Idakho. The people in Isukha and Idakho saw Kefa Ayub Mavuru as the natural successor of Solomon, whereas those in Maragoli wanted the new leader to be a man from their own area. Kefa Ayub Mavuru was elected and some people from north Maragoli now allege that there were irregularities connected with his election. According to them, no proper committee of the whole Church was set up to decide who should succeed Solomon. A committee consisting only of people from Isukha and Idakho decided in great haste that Kefa should take over. The sub-chief in Mavuru's area was involved in the decision and it had already been made by the time of Solomon's funeral. This, according to them, was an irregular procedure: the Church ought to elect its own leaders without interference from local government officers, and the whole Church ought to be involved in such an election (interview with Petro Sida and Zebedaioh Malolo, 14 June 1975; Keverenge et al. n.d.).

But when the north Maragoli people tried to find a candidate from their own area, they were unable to agree among themselves and therefore yielded, though grudgingly, to Mavuru's leadership. Much the same thing happened in 1957 when Mavuru registered the Church under the name of the African Church of Holy Spirit. The people in Maragoli say that their dissatisfaction had to do with his choice of a name for the Church.

They found, so they say, that the use of the words 'Holy Spirit' in the name constituted an act of discrimination against other Churches, in that it implied that these others, for instance the Friends, did not have the Holy Spirit. They wanted to use the name originally given to them by members of the Friends Africa Mission, namely 'Lyahuka'. But again, the Maragoli people were unable to agree on the formation of a separate Church, and they therefore continued as members of what was now the African Church of Holy Spirit. Keverenge Atonya expresses the relationship between the Isukha–Idakho section of the Church and the Maragoli section as 'two groups in one'. For practical purposes they were registered under one name, but in reality the people in Maragoli regarded their group as a separate Church (interviews with Eliakim Keverenge Atonya, 28 December 1974 and 2 January 1975).

The main reason why north Maragoli did not register as a separate Church seems to have been personal disagreements between Keverenge Atonya and his group and the people at Endeli. Endeli had been the centre of the activities of the Holy Spirit movement in north Maragoli from the beginning in 1927. This apparently made the people there feel that they had a special status and that they were the leaders of the movement in the whole of north Maragoli. However, Keverenge Atonya had also joined the Holy Spirit movement at an early date and, as time passed, his group grew larger than the one at Endeli, possibly because of better-educated leaders.

When Shem Ajega was elected to be Solomon Ahindukha's deputy in 1946, the headquarters of the north Maragoli section of the Church was placed, not at Endeli, but at Ikuvu, which was the centre of Keverenge Atonya's group (Keverenge et al. n.d.). This made the Endeli people feel that Keverenge Atonya had broken away from their leadership (interview with Enis Kadali, 23 March 1975) and relations between the two groups became tense. Then, when it came to the question of finding a leader who could stand for all Holy Spirit people in north Maragoli, the two groups were unable to agree.

The situation became worse when in the early 1960s Mavuru appointed Keverenge Atonya official leader of the north Maragoli quarterly meeting under the African Church of Holy Spirit. By that time both Joseph Chegero and Daudi Sagida, the two original leaders at Endeli, had died. The only old leader left was Enis Kadali, but people could not accept a woman as the head of their group. Many had therefore joined Keverenge Atonya's group, and the number left at Endeli had become very small. When Keverenge Atonya was now appointed to be the leader of the whole of north Maragoli, it was brought out into the open that Endeli's leading position was no longer recognized by the Church to which it officially belonged, and this caused Enis Kadali to look for new ways to assert her independence (interview with Enis Kadali, 23 March 1975).

For a number of years, therefore, both before and after the registration of the African Church of Holy Spirit, there was dissatisfaction among the members in north Maragoli. They were unhappy about the official leadership of their Church. They regarded Mavuru as the true leader of Isukha only and saw his leadership over Maragoli as essentially illegal. North Maragoli, to them, constituted an independent branch of the Holy Spirit movement, which had only submitted to the Isukha authority for practical, organizational reasons. Traditional feelings about the independence of one tribe over another can easily be observed in this matter, but another issue also came to play an important role in the relationship between the headquarters of the African Church of Holy Spirit and its members in north Maragoli, namely rivalries between different sections within north Maragoli. Though the Endeli group believed it held the leadership of the Maragoli people, the Ikuvu section of the Church gradually increased in numbers and assumed the position that had formerly belonged to Endeli. This resulted in jealousy between the leaders of the two sections and made it impossible for the Maragoli people to join hands in their opposition against the top leadership in Isukha. When the leader at Ikuvu was appointed a quarterly-meeting leader in the African Church of Holy Spirit, it became obvious that the Endeli people had lost their influence over Church matters. This caused the 'mother' of the Endeli meeting to seek independence for her group, probably assuming that Endeli would thereby regain the important position it had held during the early years of the Holy Spirit movement.

Separation in North Maragoli: Gospel Holy Spirit of East Africa
Endeli had been the centre of the Holy Spirit movement in north Maragoli for a number of years since 1927, and Enis Kadali was the first person there to receive the Spirit. With Joseph Chegero and her husband, Daudi Sagida, she had built up the congregation, and it was natural that in her view Endeli would continue to stand as the most important place for the movement in north Maragoli. Like all other Holy Spirit congregations, Endeli had taken part in the loosely knit fellowship between the movement's different groups. Enis Kadali had therefore had connections with, among others, Kefa Ayub Mavuru and Eliakim Keverenge Atonya. She had regarded their visits as recognition that Endeli was the centre of the movement, but from their point of view no such recognition was involved. They merely saw them as a way of practising fellowship on a friendly basis. When north Maragoli's headquarters were moved to Ikuvu in 1946 and the African Church of Holy Spirit registered in 1957, neither Keverenge Atonya nor Mavuru

saw these events as any kind of break, but as a natural and necessary development. To Enis Kadali, however, they appeared as if the two were consciously separating themselves and their followers from the authority of the leaders at Endeli. Until her husband died in 1958 this had not led to any crisis, for he was still the leader in his own place and had a number of followers. But when he died members left Endeli to join Mavuru's or Keverenge Atonya's groups because they could not accept a woman as their leader and her son was regarded as too young to take over his father's leadership role. What had already happened some years before therefore assumed importance at that time for Enis Kadali and the followers who were still loyal to her. They were forced to recognize that Mavuru and Keverenge Atonya had established strong groups and that they themselves were now left without a leader. Enis had to accept the reality of the situation and, to use her own words, she 'gave Kefa the meeting'. In other words, she and her followers had no choice but to submit to Mavuru's leadership, although they did this only as a matter of sheer necessity (interview with Enis Kadali, 23 March 1975).

However, Enis Kadali did not give up her wish to re-establish Endeli as the centre of the Holy Spirit movement. She wanted her own family to resume the leadership it had held when her husband was still alive. As mentioned before, the appointment of Eliakim Keverenge Atonya to the post of quarterly-meeting leader for north Maragoli within the African Church of Holy Spirit brought home even more clearly that Endeli had lost its former importance in the Holy Spirit movement. This seems to have been the provocation Enis Kadali needed and, shortly after Keverenge Atonya had become the quarterly-meeting leader, she persuaded her son to seek government registration for their Church (interview with Enis Kadali, 23 March 1975).

Her intention was to get as large a group as possible of the Holy Spirit people in north Maragoli behind her in this move, and at first there appear to have been discussions between the Endeli group and Keverenge Atonya, aimed at forming an independent Church for the whole of north Maragoli. But when the question of the leadership of the new Church came up, the people at Endeli formed their own committee, which decided that Elfas Ojiango Sagida, Enis's son, was to become its leader. And when Keverenge Atonya discovered the intentions of the Endeli people, he immediately withdrew his support from the plans. This happened at the last moment and, apparently without realizing what had happened, Elfas and his supporters went ahead and registered their Church, for which they had chosen the name 'Gospel Holy Spirit of East Africa' or, in Luragoli, *Evangeli ya Roho Mtakatifu*, with Elfas as the 'chairman'. This happened in 1964, but it soon became clear that most of the Holy Spirit people had followed Keverenge Atonya, and the Endeli group found itself left with only about ten village meetings (interview with Petro Sida, 22 March 1975).[9]

Since its registration, the Gospel Holy Spirit of East Africa has become even smaller. A number of its members have left to join larger and more active Churches, such as the African Church of Holy Spirit, the Holy Spirit Church of East Africa, the Lyahuka Church of East Africa, or the Pentecostal Church (interview with Thomas Malongo, 7 March 1975). It is not only the small number of members that has contributed to this movement out of the Church, but also its poor leadership. The chairman has migrated away from Maragoli and now lives at a settlement scheme near Lugari. From there he comes to Maragoli a few times a year, but the distance is too far for him to exercise any real influence over his Church. His mother and brother are the only members still living at Endeli, and the rest of the members are scattered in four or five village meetings (interview with Nathan Keya, 1 March 1975). The *Kenya Churches Handbook* (Barrett et al. 1973: 186) puts the adult membership of this Church at 288. But that number is obviously too high. The number who come for church services rarely exceeds 20 grown-ups, and most often it will be less than that, so my estimate is that there are about 50 adult members. Most of these are elderly, so it appears that the Church is on the point of dying.

It is obvious that an important reason for Enis Kadali's wish to establish an independent Church was her ambition to keep the leadership of the north Maragoli Holy Spirit people in her family. This ambition, combined with her limited understanding of those parts of the Holy Spirit Church that lay outside her own place and

---

9. The name Impaka is sometimes used instead of Endeli to designate where the headquarters of the Gospel Holy Spirit of East Africa are situated.

of the background of other people's claims to leadership, led her to persuade her son to register a Church that proved to be too weak to keep a hold on its members. Some tribalism was involved in this decision, for in her view it was important that north Maragoli become independent of the Isukha leadership of the African Church of Holy Spirit. Even the traditional division of society into small clan units appears to have played a role, in that, from her point of view, the small group of Holy Spirit people centred on Endeli represented the whole of north Maragoli. These factors made Enis Kadali feel justified in setting up an independent Church. And she does not regard her Church as separatist. She says that those who separated were Mavuru and Keverenge Atonya. She only made her son register their Church when the others had broken away from her, so that registration merely confirmed what was already a fact. What she did was secure official recognition for the original Church, the Church that held on to the original headquarters, to the original leaders and to the original date for the monthly meeting.

Separation in North Maragoli: Lyahuka Church of East Africa
As mentioned above, many of the Holy Spirit people in north Maragoli were dissatisfied with certain aspects of the African Church of Holy Spirit. Since the early 1930s Isukha and Idakho had held their monthly meetings on the 20th of every month while, like the Friends, Maragoli had held its on the 30th. When Kefa Ayub Mavuru succeeded Solomon Ahindukha as overall leader of the Church, the people in north Maragoli were disappointed that they had not appointed someone from their own area and alleged that there had been irregularities in the election. Furthermore, when Mavuru registered the Church as the African Church of Holy Spirit, the north Maragoli people again felt that they had been left out of the decision-making process, and their discontent was reflected in their objection to the name chosen for the Church.

Despite feeling that the Isukha leadership had been imposed on them against their will, members of the north Maragoli branch of the Holy Spirit movement submitted to Mavuru's leadership for a number of years. As we have seen, this was largely because disagreements among the Maragoli people themselves made it impossible for them to gather around any single leader. Also, Kefa Ayub

Mavuru had appointed Eliakim Keverenge Atonya, who had a fairly large following in north Maragoli and was popular among the dissatisfied elements, to leadership positions in the African Church of Holy Spirit. In the early 1960s he became north Maragoli's quarterly-meeting leader and this no doubt helped keep the discontent in the area under control. With their most important spokesman in a prominent post in the Church hierarchy, feelings of discontent were unlikely to be voiced very vehemently, for that would endanger Keverenge Atonya's position in the Church.

From Keverenge Atonya's own point of view, being the quarterly-meeting leader for the whole of north Maragoli must have seemed a satisfactory solution to the leadership problem, especially given that the people of the area had been unable to agree to the formation of an independent Church headed by him. Although the overall leadership of the African Church of Holy Spirit was placed in Isukha, he was recognized by that Church as the leader of all the north Maragoli members. Under the circumstances, this was the arrangement that could best satisfy his leadership ambitions. But Keverenge Atonya still looked upon the African Church of Holy Spirit as an organizational set-up embracing two different groups under one head. So long as he was recognized as the leader of one of those groups, the arrangement was acceptable. But as soon as this was no longer the case, the unity of the Church had to be broken.

That situation arose in 1970. The African Church of Holy Spirit had now grown so large that it became desirable to set up 'areas', units that would comprise a number of quarterly meetings. Each area was to be headed by an area superintendent who would act as a link between the headquarters and the quarterly-meeting leaders. The first area to be organized in this way was Vihiga, which came to include the quarterly meetings of north and south Maragoli together with the congregations in the Tiriki and Bunyore locations (interview with Peter Ihaji, 25 June 1975). Eliakim Keverenge Atonya had expected to be appointed as the area superintendent, but the election committee came out in favour of Harun Kereda, who was both younger and better educated than Eliakim (interview with Kefa Ayub Mavuru, 10 June 1975).

This proved to be the decisive point for Eliakim. There was now a man above him who would have more power than he in matters concerning north Maragoli. He no longer felt any loyalty to a

Church in which his claim to the top leadership of that area was not recognized. The reason given by Keverenge Atonya himself for his decision to let the split between north Maragoli and Isukha come out into the open is that in 1970 Kefa Ayub Mavuru wanted to force all meetings of his Church to hold their monthly meetings on the 20th (Keverenge et al. n.d.). Since this matter of the correct date for monthly meetings had been an issue between the two groups since the early 1930s, it appears that the real reason behind the final break was that Keverenge Atonya wanted to stand as the top leader of north Maragoli, and he was unwilling to remain in a Church in which he could no longer hold that position.

One of Eliakim Keverenge Atonya's followers, Daniel Mung'ore, had already registered a small independent Church in Nairobi in 1962 under the name of the Church of Quakers in Africa. The reason for his split from the African Church of Holy Spirit seems to have been that he wanted to be in full control of the group of followers he had gathered in Nairobi without having to submit to Mavuru's authority (interview with Javan Kasei, 4 January 1975). He had probably also expected people in Maragoli to join his Church, but they did not want a Church with headquarters in Nairobi and he was therefore left with a very small congregation. In 1965 he changed the name of his Church to the African Church of Red Cross, probably in an attempt to get Maragoli people to support him, for one of the reasons they had given for not joining him in 1962 was that they did not want the name 'Quaker'. This did not, however, help and in 1970, when Eliakim Keverenge Atonya decided to break away from the African Church of Holy Spirit, Daniel had only a very small group of supporters in Nairobi (interview with Jotham Eshera, 13 April 1975).

Keverenge Atonya now approached Daniel in an attempt to get him to join the new Church he wanted to form. And Daniel, who could see that his Church was dying, agreed to cooperate with him. Registration of the new Church therefore took the form of registering a change of name for Mung'ore's Church, and this happened in 1971. It was now called the 'Lyahuka Church of East Africa', and its headquarters were placed at Ikuvu. Eliakim Keverenge Atonya became bishop, while Daniel Mung'ore got the title of assistant bishop (Keverenge et al. n.d.).

This Church is more vigorous than the Gospel Holy Spirit of East Africa. Keverenge Atonya's original supporters followed him in his separation from the African Church of Holy Spirit. So did a number of former leaders in that Church, and it was therefore possible for him to organize the congregations of the Lyahuka Church of East Africa in very much the same way as they had been in the original Church. The *Kenya Churches Handbook* says that the total Christian community in this Church is 100 (Keverenge et al. n.d.: 186). But this number is definitely too low. The Lyahuka Church of East Africa has official branches in south Nyanza and Nairobi. There are three monthly meetings in north Maragoli, and a number of members live in Uganda and scattered in settlement schemes and other places (interviews with Manoah Lumwagi, 17 February 1975, and Jotham Eshera, 8 March 1975). Jotham Eshera says that the Church has 1200 members (interview with Jotham Eshera, 29 April, 1975), and my estimate is that this number is about right.

The Lyahuka Church of East Africa does not differ from the African Church of Holy Spirit in doctrinal matters. Nor has it set up any new system of organization. Like the Gospel Holy Spirit of East Africa, it appears to be very much the same type of Church as the one from which it broke. Keverenge Atonya, however, points out certain differences from the African Church of Holy Spirit. He says that his Church has gone back to the original custom of the Friends Church of holding the monthly meeting on the 30th of every month. Also, the name 'Holy Spirit' was discriminatory against other Churches, including the Friends, because it implied that they did not have the Spirit. He chose the name 'Lyahuka' for his Church because this was the name originally used by Friends when talking about the Holy Spirit people (interview with Eliakim Keverenge Atonya, 28 December 1974). To him, these differences from the African Church of Holy Spirit constitute an important return to the ways of the Friends Church. Sundkler (1970: 176) points out that those Churches in South Africa that separate from already existing independent Churches often rationalize their break by saying that they want to return to orthodoxy. This same phenomenon can be observed in the Lyahuka Church of East Africa. Minor matters that were of little consequence before the separation assume important proportions after it as explanations for the necessity of the split, which in reality took place for different reasons.

The real causes of Keverenge Atonya's separation seem to have been tribalism and personal ambition. The people of north Maragoli did not like being led by a man from Isukha. The independence of their own area was regarded as more important than the unity of the Church. As long as their leader was recognized as such by the headquarters of the Church, the practical arrangement whereby their area formed one branch under the Isukha headquarters was acceptable, though there were complaints that money collected in Maragoli was being sent to Isukha to help finance the headquarters (interview with Jotham Eshera, 13 April 1975). But when Keverenge Atonya came to the point of wanting to break away from the African Church of Holy Spirit because his ambition to be the top leader for north Maragoli was no longer satisfied by that Church, his followers joined him willingly.

This again corresponds to Sundkler's observations in South Africa, where he considers that the question of Church money, the struggle for power and tribal issues are among the main causes of secessions from independent Churches. Turner (1967a: 98) also mentions personal ambition as an important factor in the formation of new Churches, and Peel (1968: 276) points out that, 'paradoxically, secession is possible, and reunion difficult, because doctrine is *not* important.' He sees secession in independent Churches as a parallel to the segmentation of lineages in traditional society. In such segmentations no 'doctrinal' questions were involved, but they took place because of personal disputes. The same is seen to be the case in the separation of one Church from another, which is why it is difficult to reunite Churches once secession has taken place.

Applying Peel's theory to the Churches that have broken away from the African Church of Holy Spirit, it will be seen that because the splits followed clan and tribal lines and were dictated by personal ambition rather than doctrinal issues, there is today hardly any connection between the original Church and the two secessionist groups. There have been attempts by the general secretary of the East Africa Yearly Meeting of Friends to bring the parties together. But because personal matters are so deeply involved in the issue, he has failed to succeed.

It will be seen that the reasons why the Holy Spirit movement started in the first place are to an extent still relevant. Pressures from a rapidly changing society made many people withdraw from the world into small groups that could give them a feeling of security. The outpouring of the Holy Spirit gave them an opportunity to separate themselves from the missionaries, the agents of change. At the same time, the purifying experience of receiving the Spirit provided them with the necessary relief from their social situation. Society is still changing, and many people still need to be relieved of the pressures caused by the changes. While the same reasons that led to the start of the Holy Spirit movement nearly 50 years ago still make it attractive to a large number of people today, the movement has had to undergo many changes. At the beginning the Holy Spirit people believed that the end of the world was imminent, and therefore they made no attempts to organize their movement. Leadership was not regarded as important. All of them had fellowship with each other, and they did not try to structure the movement according to different areas. But as time passed and it became clear that the end of the world was not as near as they had thought, the Holy Spirit people had to make adjustments to society. Organization gradually assumed importance, and it was natural that the movement would often be structured along traditional lines, that is along clan or tribal lines.

The question of leadership came to the fore because, by necessity, the various branches of the movement now needed leaders. But leadership was important for other reasons too. Lonsdale (1964: 271) points out that the men who became leaders of independent Churches had often been excluded from the colonial leadership system. They were men with some education who, for various reasons, could not be absorbed into that system. An alternative for them was to become leaders of independent Churches. Welbourn (1961: 202) and Sangree (1966: xxx) interpret the question of leadership in much the same way. Sangree believes that such groups provide a transitional link between traditional and modern leadership patterns. An independent Church leader has to care for all aspects of his followers' lives, much like a traditional clan head, while at the same time representing them to the outside world, which forces him to adjust to the system of leadership accepted there. The people who fit the requirements of an independent Church leader have some education and therefore some understanding of society at large, but not enough education to set them apart from the people they are to lead. Japhet Zale Ambula and Kefa Ayub Mavuru fit the leadership pattern described by Sangree: their functions cover the same areas as those of a clan head, while at the same time they represent their Churches to the government and other people. A number of men with abilities as leaders were, and are, excluded from the government's leadership system, often because they have insufficient education, but there are numerous people who could become leaders of independent Churches. Hence the constant rivalries for the positions offered by the Churches and, as seen above, this may lead to secessions from already existing Churches.

These people do not apparently look at the formation of new Churches as breaking the principle of the unity of the Church. Sundkler (1963: 30) believes that an important reason for this is that Christianity has from the beginning been presented to them through a variety of missions. In North Kavirondo there were already four different missions before 1905 and, as we have seen, the Pentecostal Assemblies of Canada and the Salvation Army were soon added to this number. For the people of this area, the existence of different Churches must therefore appear natural. When feelings about the importance of one's own tribal or clan group and of one's own abilities as a leader cause someone to form yet another Church, this is not regarded as a violation against the basic unity of the Church. On the contrary, as in the cases of the Gospel Holy Spirit of East Africa and the Lyahuka Church of East Africa, the leaders of such secessions will often claim to be more 'original' or more 'orthodox' than the Church from which they have broken. In their own view, therefore, they bring the Church one step closer to its original unity.

So long as the conditions that cause the formation of independent Churches continue, further secessions from mission Churches and from other independent Churches can be expected to take place. Because of rapid changes in society there are still many people who feel a need for the intimate relationships and purifying experiences provided by Churches such as the four studied here. And the men with leadership aspirations, who are formed by the same society, will therefore in most cases be able to secure a following, especially among members of their own clan or tribal group.

2. Worship in the Holy Spirit Churches

Pattern of Church Services

Visitors to Holy Spirit churches will be impressed by the atmosphere of joy they meet at a church service. People sing in a very lively manner, often clapping their hands to mark the rhythm, and in many cases there will be drums, rattles and other instruments to lead the rhythmic singing. After two or three songs many people will stand and dance, or jump to the music. Eventually the whole congregation may join in the movement, and it will now easily develop into great excitement, with a number of people shouting and speaking in tongues while running around or rolling on the floor.

When coming to church services, all members wear white church uniforms with red crosses in front. Women have white headdresses, again with red crosses sewn onto them, and the men wear white turbans. Many take their turbans off inside the church to follow the rule from 1. Corinthians 11:4 and 7 which says that a man ought not to pray or to prophesy with his head covered (interviews with Japhet Zale Ambula, 2 May 1975, and Eliakim Keverenge Atonya, 27 June 1975). They also remove their shoes before entering the church. This is said to be a sign of humility before God, and in this they follow the example of Moses when he took off his shoes in front of the burning bush (Exodus 3:5; interview with the same persons). Most likely a practical consideration also plays a role in upholding this custom, namely that dancing and moving around is done more freely without shoes. The movement of many people, all in white, gives the impression of a closely knit group who, with all their individual expressions of the presence of the Holy Spirit, basically adhere to the same pattern.

This impression proves to be true when the pattern of church services is studied. At first sight, the meeting appears relatively unstructured. Anybody who feels so inclined can apparently stand up and start a song, after which the rest will join in. People move to the rhythm of the songs, they receive the Holy Spirit and roll around, uttering unintelligible or incoherent sounds. There are loud prayers with everybody speaking at the same time, but in different words, so that all that can be heard is a great noise. There is preaching, mostly by the leaders. But there are a number of leaders, and many of them may speak in the course of the same church service. Whenever somebody is preaching or praying, the congregation will respond to him, saying 'yeh' or repeating what he has said. 'Hallelujah' is shouted many times during a meeting, and people answer 'Hallelujah' enthusiastically. Whatever is done at the church service appears to the visitor who is there for the first time to happen spontaneously. People seem to do as the Spirit moves them, uncontrolled by fixed liturgical patterns.

But after having attended a few services in the Holy Spirit churches the visitor will soon discover that what at first sight appeared to happen spontaneously does indeed follow a pattern, and a rather fixed one at that. The sequence of the various elements of the service is approximately the same from one meeting to another, and each one of them is carried out in much the same way every time.

A church service normally consists of the following elements. When people enter the church they kneel and pray individually, but aloud, to prepare themselves for the service. After that there are a number of hymns and then it is time to chase all evil out of the church with clapping and shouting. Then there is individual purification during which each person confesses his or her sins, asks for forgiveness and chases out the evil. These are the opening stages of the service. Having thus cleansed the church and themselves of evil the Holy Spirit people then proceed with the business of the meeting. Prayers are led by one or more of the elders and everybody says the Lord's Prayer, often several times. After several more hymns those who have had dreams or visions may stand up and tell them to the congregation. And then, after more songs, an elder interprets the dreams and visions. There are more hymns, a collection is taken and a prayer is said for the collection. After more songs everybody kneels and recites in a chorus Psalms 1 and 25, and possibly also the Ten Commandments and the Apostles' Creed. One or two preachers often support their message with the singing of certain well-known hymns. There may be prayers for specific groups of people and for specific problems, and the meeting ends with another chasing out of all evil and with prayer.

Not all these elements appear at every church service, though most of them normally do. Although a certain programme exists and the elders try to lead the meeting according to it, it is seen only as a guideline. The Holy Spirit is the real leader of the meeting, so the elders must take care not to impose a programme; they must leave space for the Spirit to conduct the meeting (interview with Timotheo Hezekiah Shitsimi, 6 June 1976). The freedom of the Spirit is illustrated by the trances that may appear at various stages of the service, for instance after a number of hymns or after a preaching. When people are seized by the Spirit they perform convulsive movements, roll around, shout and speak in tongues.

Because the Spirit cannot be controlled by a fixed programme, only a few of the elements mentioned above have to appear at any given service. In my observation, the elements that are always present are hymn singing, chasing out evil, confession and prayer, including the Lord's Prayer. Timotheo Hezekiah Shitsimi's list of necessary elements is slightly different. He says that singing, confession and the Lord's Prayer are obligatory, but in addition mentions the collection and the recital of Psalms 1 and 23 and of the Apostles' Creed as indispensable.

Though Shitsimi stresses the importance of the Apostles' Creed, I have never heard it recited in his Church, the African Church of Holy Spirit. But members of the Lyahuka Church of East Africa say it as a chorus at nearly all meetings, possibly adhering to an old custom which, though regarded as important, has practically disappeared from use in the African Church of Holy Spirit.

There are other differences between the four Churches studied here. They follow the same general pattern for the conduct of their meetings, but there are variations in emphasis. The most conspicuous differences are that the Holy Spirit Church of East Africa spends a larger part of the service on prayer than the other Churches. The African Church of Holy Spirit seems to have developed the purification elements further than the others, although in this respect the difference is not quite as pronounced as it is concerning prayer. Also, in this Church members enter trances and speak in tongues at normal services more often than they do in the three other Churches.

It will be seen, therefore, that the four Holy Spirit Churches follow basically the same pattern in their church services. There are variations in emphasis from one Church to another, but the same fundamental elements are to be found in all of them, The free movement of the Spirit is still seen as the principle underlying all that is done at a service. But in practice, the expressions of the Spirit's guidance have come to adhere to relatively fixed rules. In what follows, the most important elements in the worship of the Holy Spirit Churches will be described in more detail.

The Importance of Hymns
The main impression of a service in one of the Holy Spirit Churches is that people are happy and that they want to give praise to God through their activities during the meeting. Their hymns, and especially their manner of singing them, is one of the most important ways in which they can express their joy and thankfulness.

A very large number of hymns is in use in these Churches, and they come from various sources. But the two main sources are the Friends' Luragoli hymn book and the Holy Spirit Churches themselves. Without having counted the exact ratio between these two kinds of hymns, my estimate is that each of them takes up about half the time used for singing at any given service, occasionally with a few songs from the Salvation Army, the Pentecostal Church and the Church of God added.

Since these Churches originated in the Friends Africa Mission, they have naturally taken over a number of the hymns used by that mission. But the manner in which they are sung by the Holy Spirit people is very different from that found in a Friends church. While the Friends sing in a slow, quiet manner, these people clap, dance and jump to the Friends songs, just as they do to their own original hymns, thereby completely transforming the character of the songs.

In the Friends Church, hymns are what Sundkler calls 'a versified statement about certain religious facts'. He finds that African independent Churches change the character of hymns, so that the statement of religious facts is no longer the main purpose in the singing of hymns, as it was in the mission Churches. Instead, they become 'sacred rhythm' (Sundkler 1970: 196). The clapping, the rhythmic movements and the repetition of whole songs or of their choruses in the Holy Spirit Churches do indeed add an important new dimension to the Friends hymns. They no longer serve only the purpose of giving the teachings of the Church. They are also the means of expressing the Church members' joy and praise to the Lord, and through them the feelings of the congregation can gradually rise to the point where they enter a trance and thereby reach the highest stage of communion with God. In this way, the hymns from the Friends Church have become incorporated into the worship of the Holy Spirit Churches. The main aim of the services in these Churches is to experience the presence of the Spirit and to give thanks for this gift, and all hymns, both those from the Friends Church and those that have their origin in the Holy Spirit Churches, serve that purpose.

Their own original hymns are built up in such a way that they fit directly into the pattern of rhythmic singing. Church members claim they all come from the Holy Spirit. A specially gifted person may have received them in a dream or vision, but even in the course of a church service a new tune and new words may develop gradually, with the participation of everybody, so that no particular person can be pointed out as the author (Sundkler 1970). Their own hymns normally take up only one theme, which is repeated with small variations, the most important part of them being the chorus, which may be sung over and over again. One of the most popular original hymns is the following:

> *Bali nobugasu yavo vasalanga. (3 times)*
> *Va Yesu mwene yavavolela.*
> *Chorus:*
> *Haleluya Haleluya (3 times)*
> *Lwa Yesu mwene yavavolela.*

English translation:

> *They are blessed those who pray. (3 times)*
> *Jesus himself has told them.*
> *Chorus:*
> *Hallelujah Hallelujah (3 times)*
> *When Jesus himself has told them.*

The subsequent verses differ from the first only in the last word of the first line. 'Those who pray' is replaced by 'those who believe', 'those who repent', 'those who preach', 'those who confess' and so on. This simple, repetitive structure makes the original hymns very suitable for the kind of singing which, with the help of rhythm marked by clapping and drumming, can gradually build up an emotional atmosphere and bring people into trances.

Hymns can be introduced at any point in a church service, for hymn singing occurs whenever the meeting moves from one stage to another. One of the song leaders, usually a woman, stands up and shouts 'Hallelujah' a number of times, to which the congregation answers 'Hallelujah'. After this introduction she starts the song of her choice, and the others soon join in. No hymn books are used; everybody knows the songs by heart, or at least the choruses. Since there is no rule about who should lead the various songs, two people sometimes stand up at the same time and start two different songs. The confusion is always quickly sorted out. It is accepted that both have felt led by the Spirit and therefore the solution is for one to sit down and wait until the song has finished, after which she will lead the next song.

Hymns are not always sung in this lively manner. When people kneel down to pray they often sing a hymn, usually one taken over from the Friends Church, and then there is no clapping. They sing in a calm, quiet way. The hymn thus takes on the character of a prayer or an exhortation to pray earnestly in the belief that the prayer which is to follow will be answered. Sometimes it may also serve as a confession of faith before the prayer begins.

Finally, hymns can be used by a preacher to support a point he wants to emphasize. He then starts the hymn himself, after which he continues his sermon. This illustrates another important function of the hymns. They are, after all, 'versified statements' about the teachings of the Church. Although they serve other purposes as well, the essential role played by hymns in the teaching of Church doctrines must not be overlooked.

It appears, then, that hymns serve the edification of the congregation on both the emotional and intellectual levels. Joseph Mahasi (1974) describes the difference between African and Western religious expressions in that he says that African worship is 'celebrational of life', whereas Western worship is 'meditational and reflective'. Leaving out the question of whether this contrast can be upheld in all cases, it is true that for the Holy Spirit people, the Friends Church services offered little emotional stimulation. And when they formed their own Churches, they developed a pattern of worship which would give each member a chance to participate actively and thereby to experience his own worth in the eyes of God, with whom he would feel in close communion. Mahasi (1974) says, 'We have therefore to dance Christianity, to shout Christianity to sing Christianity, to act Christianity, to drum Christianity with all our being.'

The action, the 'sacred rhythm' aspect of the hymn singing, is a celebration of life, of these people's experience of unity with God and of fellowship with each other, an experience which assumes great importance for people who are placed in a situation of social change where traditional relationships have been disrupted. But what they dance, what they shout, and what they sing is exactly Christianity. Theirs is a Church and not just any social group, and therefore the teaching aspect of the hymns is as important as the action aspect. Through the words of the hymns these people are taught about the God with whom they experience community through the rhythm of the same hymns.

Purification Rituals

Shortly after a church service has begun, when a number of hymns have been sung, there is a ritual for chasing all evil out of the church. A priest runs a few steps down the middle of the church, shouting, 'All evil that wants to spoil the meeting — *Gi twulidzwe!* All demons — *Gi twulidzwe!*' When he shouts '*Gi twulidzwe!*' he claps his hands in the direction of the door, which has been opened to allow all the evil to leave the church (interview with Eliakim Keverenge Atonya, 27 June 1975). The congregation stand, turned towards the door, and join the priest in clapping and shouting '*Gi twulidzwe*'.

Gi twulidzwe! means 'may it be taken away' in Luragoli. The plural form, *vi twulidzwe*, is the Luragoli translation of ἀρθήτω — in Ephesians 4:31 (interview with Japhet Zale Ambula, 2 May 1975).[1] It is not a secret word like those used by the Church of

---

1. The English translation reads: 'Let all bitterness and wrath and anger and clamour and slander *be put away* from you, with all malice.' (Emphasis added. These are the words that are translated into '*vi twulidzwe*' in Luragoli.)

the Lord in West Africa, which are regarded as particularly powerful precisely because they are not found in normal language
(Turner 1967b). *Gi twulidzwe* is a normal word in the Luyia
languages. But its use in church services, where it is always this
particular word that is shouted to drive out evil and where it is
used repeatedly, suggests that it has assumed the same function as
the secret words in the Church of the Lord. It has become a kind
of 'spiritual magic' (Turner 1967b: 72), powerful enough to drive
out demons.

After this collective purification ritual comes personal purification. Before the meeting can be pure and before it can proceed
to pray, praise God and seek the outpouring of the Holy Spirit, all
the congregants have to confess all their sins openly. In the early
days of the Holy Spirit movement people would stand up individually and confess their sins, but nowadays the normal procedure is for everybody in the church to confess at the same time.
It is still an open confession because they speak aloud, but when
everybody does it at the same time all that can be heard is a great
noise, and nobody is able to tell exactly what sins each individual
has committed. People stand and swing their arms back and forth
and move their bodies while confessing, and in between they say,
'*Yesu yasamehe*', 'may Jesus forgive me', or '*Gi twulidzwe*'.

An indication that some people regard these words as 'spiritual
magic' is that a special word, *osiwigisu*, can often be heard during
confessions. This word does not mean anything; it is nothing but a
mistaken form of *yasamehe Yesu*, which, when pronounced fast,
can develop into *osiwigisu*. But this shows that people do not
think too deeply about the meaning of the words they use to ask
Jesus to forgive them. Instead, *Yesu yasamehe* or *osiwigisu*, like *gi
twulidzwe*, becomes a fixed formula for helping to drive out the
demons that cause people to commit sins.

An additional style of personal confession has been developed
in the African Church of Holy Spirit and the Lyahuka Church of
East Africa in which, instead of everybody standing up at the same
time and saying whatever they like, a priest mentions the various
types of sins. For instance, he may say, 'Repent your sins concerning children,' or 'Repent your sins that have to do with bicycles.'
Those who feel they have something to confess in connection with
the item just mentioned will stand up and confess in the way
described above. But those who are not concerned with that par-

ticular sin will remain seated. The priest will then mention another sin, and again some will stand up and confess while the others wait until something that concerns them is mentioned. This may go on for quite a long time, with everybody confessing to a number of sins. Although the priest raises the subjects about which people are to confess, his description is kept so general that nobody knows the exact nature of someone else's sin. According to Timotheo Hezekiah Shitsimi (interview, 6 June 1976), this type of confession is used when the Holy Spirit has revealed to the priest that the sins he mentions have been committed by members of the congregation. 'In this way,' he says, 'God helps us to remember our sins.' It is possible that this type of confession also reminds people that they are asking for forgiveness for sins they themselves have committed and are not just driving away impersonal evil powers with the help of magic words.

The original way of confessing, in which people stand up individually and say what sins they have committed, is still in use, but not normally at regular church services. Only if people have committed very serious sins and have been under Church discipline will they, on being accepted back into the fellowship of the Church, confess before everybody else what they have done, and all the others will then help them pray for forgiveness (interview with Timotheo Hezekiah Shitsimi, 6 June 1976). Youth services and women's meetings are other occasions for individual confession. At youth meetings the priests teach the young people how to repent, so they therefore have to confess individually (youth meeting, Chanda church of the Lyahuka Church of East Africa, 12 April 1975). Women's meetings serve the purpose of providing the women of the Church with a close fellowship within which they can do and say things they would be unable to do freely in the presence of men. Most sins associated with domestic problems are therefore confessed in these groups (information from Peter Mandwa, 25 December 1974).

Repentance and confession are also seen as important elements of Christian life in the Friends Church, but here the methods of confession are different from those found in Holy Spirit Churches. In most cases they take the form of a private confession to God without the knowledge of other church members. As seen above in Chapter 1, this way of confessing sins was, and is, regarded by the Holy Spirit people as insufficient. Only open confession can

cleanse them completely and thereby enable them to receive the
Holy Spirit.

Purification rites played an important role in the traditional
Abaluyia religion. People could become ritually impure either
through acts they themselves had committed or for reasons
beyond their control. When this happened a purification rite had
to be performed to restore the person in question to full ritual
status, and thereby avert the danger of the impurity harming either
its carrier or others. The various kinds of impurities each had their
corresponding purification rites. These often involved the use of
an animal's skin, or the contents of its stomach, or the victim
might be required to bathe in a stream to be cleansed (Wagner
1949: 106, 245).

The same purpose, purification from ritual impurity, can be
observed in the practices of the Holy Spirit Churches. Here also,
the sins people have committed, and the evil that has led them to
sin and which can also enter the church and contaminate the
whole meeting, has to be chased out to restore the ritual status
and thus allow communion with God to become possible. But
none of the traditional means of purification are employed in the
Holy Spirit Churches. Use of such means would be equivalent to
worshipping *misambwa*[2] or of 'other gods' (an expression used by
Timotheo Hezekiah Shitsimi in an interview on 6 June 1976).
Christian means are the only ones allowed. In South African
Zionist Churches and in West African Aladura (Prayer) Churches
water plays an important role in purification rites (Sundkler 1970:
200; Turner 1967b: 107). But in the Holy Spirit Churches no
external means are employed, even though water was sometimes
used in traditional purification rituals. This is probably due to
influence from the Friends tradition, which forbids water baptism
or any other outward sacramental rite. The South and West
African Churches find the justification for their water rituals in the
mission Churches' practice of water baptism. But the Holy Spirit
Churches have no such justification, which is probably why
purification in these Churches is confined to confession accom-

2. The word means 'ancestors', and in the terminology of the Holy Spirit
    Churches it stands for the whole body of traditional beliefs and
    practices. Used, for example, by Kefa Ayub Mavuru in a sermon on
    26 December 1974.

panied by bodily movements and driving demons from the church, again without the use of any outward means.

It has been seen that rituals for purification are important elements in the worship of the Holy Spirit Churches. They are used less in the Holy Spirit Church of East Africa than in the others, but in all of them they play an important role. They serve the purpose of driving out all evil from the church as such and from each individual member, thereby opening the way to communion with God. Over the years, simple confession of sin has developed into fixed rituals. But neither the customs of the Friends Church nor the purification rites in traditional religion have been copied. The Holy Spirit Churches have developed their own rituals for purification in which the same symbolic bodily actions accompany the same style of speaking from one meeting for worship to another.

Prayers

Once the purification rites have been performed, the meeting is free to proceed to prayer, to preaching and possibly to receiving the Holy Spirit. Without purification this would not be possible. The relationship between purification and prayer was expressed in a speech during a church service by one elder at the Lugala head-quarters of the African Church of Holy Spirit (20 March 1975) when he urged the congregation to repent before kneeling in prayer:

> If you know that you have sins and you kneel down with your sins, Christ will never come near to you. ... Therefore, repent before you kneel before God. When you kneel down while your heart is in a bad condition, God will not listen to you. Therefore, the best [thing to do] is to purify yourselves before you kneel before God.

God will only listen to people who pray to him with clean hearts, and therefore purification has to take place before prayer.

But when this has been done the congregation will kneel down while the leaders stand with their hands lifted over the heads of those below them. There will now be quiet singing of a hymn, which in this situation takes on the character of a prayer, or sometimes of an exhortation to prayer or a confession of faith in the God to whom they want to pray. Then an elder will pray on behalf of everybody and the congregation will show its participation in the prayer by answering 'yeh' or repeating the last words of each sentence. The Lord's Prayer will be recited by everybody in a chorus, often two to three times immediately after each other and sometimes more. At one service the Lord's Prayer was repeated 12 times! Here again, Turner's (1967b: 72) observation that special words or repeated prayers may serve as 'spiritual magic' seems to be relevant.

This long prayer consisting of three different elements will always take place at an early stage of the service, shortly after purification. In the African Church of Holy Spirit and the two Churches that have separated from it there will not be much more praying, except for a prayer after the collection and at the end of the meeting when everybody will stand up and raise their hands towards heaven. In the Holy Spirit Church of East Africa there will be several more prayers, often consisting again of the same three elements. And in most cases not only one, but three elders will pray each time.

During prayers the doors and windows of the church are closed. When asked for the reason for this, Church elders refer to Matthew 6:6 which reads: 'But when you pray, go into your room and shut the door and pray to your Father who is in secret; and your Father who sees in secret will reward you' (interview with Japhet Zale Ambula, 2 May 1975). Doors are also closed while people are possessed by the Holy Spirit. In both cases this appears to be for the same reason as why the doors are opened while evil powers are being driven from the church, namely that the demons were actually thought to leave the church through the door. In the case of prayer and of receiving the Spirit it seems likely that the doors and windows are closed to prevent evil spirits entering the church again and disturbing the meeting.

Looking at the contents of prayers, it will be seen that asking for forgiveness is only of minor importance, which is to be expected after such thorough purification rites. There are prayers for the defeat of enemies that threaten the congregation. But again, evil powers have already been driven out of the church and therefore the prayers do not dwell much on this element. It may be significant that more prayers for the defeat of enemies are said in the Holy Spirit Church of East Africa than in the other three

Churches, where the purification rituals are more developed. A typical prayer led by an elder will mostly ask for God to bless the meeting and be near to all the members. I quote as an example the following prayer, given by an elder in a church service at Lugala headquarters at a quarterly meeting of the African Church of Holy Spirit on 20 March 1975:

I am asking the Father, the Son and the Holy Spirit. We are here before you. The 20th meeting, I put it in your hands. Bless this meeting. Bless me. Bless us. Bless the meeting. Oh Lord God, elders are kneeling before you. Bless them. All this I put before you. All women are kneeling before you. I put all this before you. Children are kneeling before you. I put them in your hands. Everything I leave to you. All blessings should come from you. Bless the meeting. Take care of guests and bless the meeting. Bless the meeting. And bless the meeting and all that I am saying. Bless the quarterly meeting. Bless it. Bless it. Bless it. Blessings should come from your hands. Jehovah God, bless the meeting. With all your power. And your blood. With your blood. With your blood, you holy one. You who bought the meeting with your blood and with your strength. God who is the holy one. Give your holy blood. Give your holy blood. Give your holy blood. Amen.

After each sentence the congregation answered 'yeh', 'bless it', and the more the elder repeated the words of the prayer, the louder were the answers. The repetitive form of most prayers therefore serves to build up an emotional atmosphere conducive to receiving the Holy Spirit.

Some prayers are more concrete in content than the one quoted above. There may be prayers for rain and a good harvest, prayers for the sick to be healed and the barren to bear children, prayers for children to do well at school or for grown-ups to find jobs. Such prayers are heard mostly in the Holy Spirit Church of East Africa, though they do also exist in the other Churches. In the Gospel Holy Spirit of East Africa there will normally be prayers for the sick towards the end of the service, when those suffering in one way or another come to the front to be prayed for. And in all the Churches priests often go to the homes of their members to pray whenever a problem of this kind arises.

But the Holy Spirit Church of East Africa differs from the other Churches in that special prayers for people's personal problems are said at every service. Anyone is invited to stand up and mention a specific problem about which they would like the people in the church to pray. After a few have aired their problems in this way everybody begins to tell theirs, but now simultaneously so that all that can be heard is a great noise. When people quieten down again, an elder stands up and prays while the rest of the congregation kneels, and he now prays in the usual way, with others responding in between. He prays for those who first mentioned their problems and, in a general way, for whatever might have been said during the collective noise.

Undoubtedly prayers of this kind, whether said in the church or in people's homes, are of greater importance in the Holy Spirit Churches than they were in the Friends Africa Mission, where the emphasis was on repentance of sin and prayers for forgiveness. As we have seen, this has been taken over by the Holy Spirit Churches, in that cleansing from sin has become the cornerstone without which any real communion with God is regarded as being impossible. But for the faithful who have been purified God is seen as the provider of all things in life. He is the one who can bring fertility to the land and to the people, who can heal the sick and give success at school. Comparing these prayers with those said in connection with sacrifices in traditional religion, it can be understood why God is thought of as the one who will give his children everything they need, even though the mission from which these Churches originated did not emphasize that aspect very much. Wagner mentions that prayers and sacrifices in traditional religion would aim at securing health and welfare in general, and at invoking the blessing and sympathy of benevolent spirits. This corresponds to the type of prayer quoted above, where people pray for God's blessing, but not for any specific problem. In addition to these general prayers there were traditionally more specific prayers in which people would ask for help in case of illness, barrenness, cattle diseases, crop failures or other problems affecting their welfare (Wagner 1949: 279). It will be seen, therefore, that when prayers are said for specific problems which people have asked the church or their priest to pray for, there is a close parallel to the type of prayers said in traditional religion.

Prayers during services in the Holy Spirit Churches are therefore said according to a relatively fixed pattern. The normal posture during prayer, kneeling, and the lifting up of hands at the end of the meeting, may have been learnt from other Churches, for members of the Friends Church sit down while they pray. When the leaders lift their hands over the heads of the congregation it may remind the Holy Spirit people of Arthur Chilson, who lifted his hands over the heads of those at Kaimosi who had openly confessed their sins before receiving the Holy Spirit. In their content, however, the prayers clearly reflect the kinds of problems about which people prayed in traditional religion. The Holy Spirit Churches have also been influenced by the way in which prayers are said in the Friends Church, though the points emphasized in the Friends' prayers are brought out more clearly in the purification rites of these Churches than in their prayers. The form of a prayer is often repetitive, and the Lord's Prayer may be repeated a number of times. Through this repetition the feelings of the congregation gradually rise to higher emotional pitches, culminating in some cases in a number of members being seized by the Holy Spirit.

Teaching and Admonishment through Preaching
At least one person preaches at every church service, but often two or three. In principle, it is not planned beforehand who is going to speak at the service because people ought to preach only if urged to do so by the Holy Spirit. If either before or during the service someone feels called by the Spirit to preach, he or she informs whoever is in charge of the meeting, and is then given a chance to speak at an appropriate time. Alternatively, someone may receive a message from the Holy Spirit that some other person has to preach. The person in question is then informed and, in turn, will recognize this as a calling by the Spirit which has to be obeyed (interview with Timotheo Hezekiah Shitsimi, 6 June 1976).

Since the Spirit may choose any person to preach, the sermons are rarely prepared in advance. There are many examples of people who rise and begin to preach by saying, 'I did not know that I would come here today, and I do not have much to say,' and then proceed to give a long speech. This principle of the Spirit leading people to speak may also cause some to believe in the direct divine inspiration of their otherwise not very substantial sermons.

Certain leaders are often called to preach and, judging from their sermons, some of them do prepare beforehand the message they want to bring. Also, such top leaders seem to have made it a rule to speak after the other preachers and to sum up what has been said before, sometimes indirectly correcting certain points in the others' speeches and giving them a turn which, in their opinion, is more in keeping with the true Church doctrines.

Through preaching, the teachings of the Holy Spirit Churches are brought to the members, and they are urged to make up their minds to follow the God about whom they learn in this way. Most sermons place a strong emphasis on heaven and on how to get there. Members are admonished to leave the sinful ways of this world in order to secure for themselves a place in heaven when Jesus comes to call them.

There are frequent references to scripture verses; these are not usually read by the preacher himself, but by someone standing ready with a Bible at hand. In this way it becomes impossible to discern whether or not the preacher is literate, and embarrassment is avoided. Following the tradition of the Friends Church and the principle of the freedom of the Spirit there is no pericope system with fixed readings for specific days. Individual preachers choose their own themes on which to speak and the appropriate Bible verses. No parts of the Bible seem to be excluded from practical use, but certain books are particularly popular, especially the apocalyptic books of Daniel and the Revelation.

The purpose of preaching, to teach and to admonish people to follow the way to heaven, is similar to that of the Friends Church, but the style of preaching has changed. Whereas most Friends sermons are delivered in a calm, matter-of-fact way, preachers in the Holy Spirit Churches make an effort to arouse the feelings of their listeners. They move around while speaking, illustrating points they want to make by gesticulating with their arms. To hold the congregation's attention, they may vary their voices from low, nearly inaudible speech to shouting. Frequently shouting 'Hallelujah!', to which the others respond, serves the same purpose. The members of the congregation repeat important points and the speaker asks questions about what has been said, which everybody answers in a chorus. Some preachers break their sermons at certain moments to start singing a hymn to illustrate a point, and the listeners readily join in.

These techniques are more highly developed by some preachers than others, and those who seem to prepare their sermons most thoroughly are also the ones best able to keep the attention of the congregation and to move the mood of their listeners in the direction they want. When the emotional message calling people to prepare themselves to go to heaven is delivered by a preacher who understands the minds of his people, the sermon can become one of the most powerful means through which the feelings of a congregation can be stirred; this is often when they enter a trance and thereby receive assurance that God is near and that he will lead them on the way to heaven.

Preaching in Holy Spirit Churches therefore serves the same purpose as in the Friends Church and in other Churches. It is a way of teaching the Church's doctrines to its members and of admonishing them to believe in God and to follow the rules laid down by the Church. But preaching in these Churches serves another purpose as well — arousing feelings to the point of losing control and thus enabling the members of the congregation to undergo the experience of being possessed by the Holy Spirit.

Confession of Faith through the Recital of Psalms
When asked which elements are indispensable at a church service, Timotheo Hezekiah Shitsimi (interview, 6 June 1976) answered, among other things, Psalms 1 and 23 and the Apostles' Creed. When asked the same question, leaders of the Lyahuka Church of East Africa also said that at every meeting Psalms 1 and 23 must be recited by the congregation (information from leaders on 9 March 1975). And, as a matter of fact, these two psalms are heard at nearly all meetings of the two Churches and of the Gospel Holy Spirit of East Africa.

The psalms are recited by the whole congregation in a chorus, and everybody kneels while saying them. The time of the service at which they come in differs. But in many cases they are recited in connection with the purification rituals, and their use at this time shows that they have assumed the character of a confession of faith. Psalm 1 illustrates these people's conviction that if they remain righteous, as ensured through purification, they will receive God's blessings, while unbelievers will not be accepted by Him. And Psalm 23 becomes a confession of their faith that God will forever give His blessings to His faithful people.

As mentioned above, I have never heard the Apostles' Creed at a service in the African Church of Holy Spirit, although in theory it is an important element of the service. But in the Lyahuka Church of East Africa this Creed will be recited immediately after the two psalms, thereby stressing their character of confession. The Ten Commandments normally follow after the Creed, setting forth the ways of the righteous.

The Apostles' Creed, the Ten Commandments, and Psalms 1 and 23 were among the important teachings in the Friends Africa Mission, which every new convert had to learn. No doubt, the Holy Spirit Churches have learnt from the Friends the importance of these passages, which, with their emphasis on securing righteousness in the eyes of God and assurance that He will be near to His faithful people and give them His blessings, fit into the content of their services. When they recite these passages, most important of which are the psalms, the members of the Holy Spirit Churches bear witness to their faith towards each other and towards the world.

Turner mentions the extensive use of psalms in the Church of the Lord and warns that because of a lack of historical reference they 'are too easily turned into a new set of powerful Christian words whose very utterance can secure victory for the user' (Turner 1967b: 73). Such thinking probably plays a role among members of the Holy Spirit Churches also, in that they wish to secure the realization of what they confess. Therefore, the recital of psalms seems to be looked upon as confession and prayer in one. When reciting psalms the congregation kneel in the same way as they do during prayer, and this probably indicates that they are praying to God that what they profess to believe may prove to be true.

Perhaps this element of prayer in the recital of psalms is the reason why they do not appear to be important in the Holy Spirit Church of East Africa, where I have not heard them recited. As we have seen, prayers take up a larger part of the services in this Church than in the others. Also, the quiet singing of hymns while kneeling is practised more here. And since hymns sung in this way sometimes take on the character of a confession of faith, this Church may not feel any need for other kinds of confessions.

But in the other three Holy Spirit Churches Psalms 1 and 23 and sometimes the Apostles' Creed and the Ten Commandments are recited regularly, thereby showing their dependence on the Friends Church. They serve the purpose of emphasizing important points in the teachings of these Churches, namely the need to be righteous and God's promise that those who remain faithful will receive his blessings. At the same time, these recitals contain an element of prayer that what the Churches profess to believe may be proved by God to be true.

Outpouring of the Holy Spirit

At nearly all the Holy Spirit church services there are some signs of the outpouring of the Spirit in that people perform convulsive movements and speak in an incoherent manner. This may happen to a few persons only, or just about the whole congregation may be possessed by the Spirit. The principle of the freedom of the Spirit applies again here, and therefore meetings differ in this respect.

Although human beings are thought to have no power to decide whether or not the Holy Spirit descends on the congregation, there are certain things that can be done to open the way for it to come. The most important condition for receiving the Holy Spirit is purity of heart, and therefore members are urged to repent all the sins they have committed. There are special meetings at which leaders teach their people how to repent. Once they have done that, human beings can do no more. The rest is up to the Holy Spirit itself (interviews with Peter Ihaji, 25 June 1975, and Eliakim Keverenge Atonya, 27 June 1975).

As we have seen above, however, apart from repentance and the confession of sins, certain other things are done at church services to create an atmosphere conducive to an outpouring of the Spirit. Rhythmic hymn singing accompanied by clapping and sometimes by drums and other instruments, together with the repetitive style of the singing, can in many cases stir people's emotions until they lose their normal control and receive the Holy Spirit. Emotional prayers, also characterized by repetition, were seen to be able to produce the same effect, just as sermons preached in such a way as to touch the feelings of the congregation may result in strong emotional outbursts and in a state of possession.

As one might expect, therefore, the most concentrated expressions of receiving the Holy Spirit are often found towards the end

of a service when the emotional atmosphere has been built up to
sufficient heights. The congregation may continue to sing one song
after another. The dancing accompanying the singing becomes
more and more lively until people suddenly begin to roll on the
floor or stagger around speaking in tongues. Sometimes everyone
in the congregation, apart from the majority of elders, is seized by
the Spirit. The elders, who feel they ought to listen and observe
what is going on, normally remain calm throughout the meeting
(interview with Timotheo Hezekiah Shitsimi, 3 June 1976). Some
of them walk among the people rolling on the floor, sometimes
bending to listen to the words being uttered through the Spirit,
sometimes holding those who tend to become violent or who try
to move to the side of the church reserved for the opposite sex.

The belief in the Holy Spirit Churches is that the Holy Spirit
speaks through people who have entered a trance and are speaking
in tongues. Speaking in tongues is very often an expression of
happiness, and in this way people can praise God in the highest
way for what He has done for them. On the other hand, tongues
may express deep sorrow, and through this kind of speech people
may pray for God's forgiveness and for His presence in a much
more concentrated and earnest way than is possible in normal
words. Also, people who speak in tongues are thought to serve as
mediums between God and human beings. Through them the
Holy Spirit brings messages, just as it does through prophecy, but
with the difference that the message brought through a person
who speaks in tongues is not immediately understandable to most
people and has to be interpreted (interviews with Japhet Zale
Ambula, 2 May 1975, Kefa Ayub Mavuru, 10 June 1975, and
Timotheo Hezekiah Shitsimi, 3 June 1976).

The interpretation of tongues is very rarely done during a
church service. This is accounted for by two considerations. First,
God may be revealing something through the medium that would
be embarrassing to other members of the congregation, so therefore should not be said in public. Second, not only God, but Satan,
may speak through people, so what they say should not be
revealed to the church until the leaders have looked into the
contents of the message (interviews with Japhet Zale Ambula, 2
May 1975, Kefa Ayub Mavuru, 10 June 1975, and Timotheo
Hezekiah Shitsimi, 3 June 1976). This is contrary to what was
practised during the early years of the Holy Spirit movement when

there were no such restraints. But experience over the years must have shown that not everything that pretends to be of the Spirit is the true word of God.

In fact, an observer of Holy Spirit church services will sometimes get the impression that not all cases of speaking in tongues are genuine. There appears to be no pretence when the whole church is possessed in the way described above, for then the hymns or preaching preceding the trance have stirred people's emotions to the extent that the state of possession seems to come as a natural consequence. But in many cases only a few persons, or even just one, are seized by the Spirit. They will begin to shake and, in an abrupt manner, say some of the words typically used by those who speak in tongues, for instance, '*Hodi*', 'Amen', '*Mtakatifu*', '*Livukana*', or simply 'Rrrrrr', 'OK' or any other English words they might know.[3] Such persons sometimes appear insincere, to be pretending that the Holy Spirit is speaking through them, probably in an attempt to gain the attention of the group and to be recognized as a true man of God. Instead of fitting into the mood of the service such utterances often disturb the meeting by distracting people's attention from what is going on.

Pretended (as well as genuine) states of possession result from the attitude in the Holy Spirit Churches that it is desirable for everybody to receive the Spirit and to speak in tongues. Receiving the Spirit is regarded as the highest communion with God and nobody can be a true Christian without at one time or another having this experience. Never having been possessed is regarded as proof of not having confessed all one's sins, and such people are urged again and again to purify themselves (interview with Timotheo Hezekiah Shitsimi, 3 June 1976). There is therefore social pressure on people in these Churches to receive the Holy Spirit. This, combined with the emotional character of the meetings, easily creates a situation in which Spirit possession becomes the obvious way of both expressing one's religious feelings and of conforming to group expectations. But this social pressure may also lead certain people to pretend to receive the Holy Spirit in order to be fully accepted by the Church. Group expectations also

3. '*Hodi*' is what is said when knocking on somebody's door and means something like 'May I come in?' '*Mtakatifu*' means 'Holy', and '*livukana*' is 'meeting' or 'church service'.

explain how the elders are able to retain their feelings of responsibility and remain calm when the whole congregation is in a
trance.

As shown above, members of the Friends Africa Mission
reacted strongly against the outpouring of the Holy Spirit in 1927.
Although this Church believed in the Holy Spirit, it could not
accept the noisy manifestations of its presence. The ready acceptance by the Holy Spirit people of Arthur Chilson's message had
its background not in the teachings of the majority of missionaries, but in the need created by their social situation for this
purifying experience which also gave them a new feeling of their
own worth.

Spirit possession was not completely new to Luyia society. In
the traditional culture certain people became possessed by a spirit
as a sign that they had been called to take up one of the specialized 'offices', such as that of a diviner or of a rain-magician
(Wagner 1949: 156, 242). But it was something that happened to
only very few people, and there was no group spirit cult as among
many other Bantu peoples. Welbourn suggests, though, that there
is an indirect connection between these cults and the spirit possession found in the African Israel Church Nineveh, in that the
rapidly changing social structure created a need for expressions of
the kind found in the spirit cults and made the people of that
Church conform to the general Bantu pattern (Welbourn 1969:
302). Taylor and Lehmann, on the other hand, believe that the
reason why trances were uncommon in the Churches in Northern
Rhodesia is that traditionally there was a strong group spirit cult
in the area, and the Churches feared forms of expression that
might be interpreted as belonging to that cult (Taylor and
Lehmann 1961: 295). In western Kenya there was no need for
such fears since such cults did not exist there in pre-Christian
times. It is possible that one reason why the Holy Spirit movement
gained many adherents is that when social conditions made
possession a desirable experience, these people could accept it as
an element that was important in their traditional religion, but
without the features that might have caused people to see the
Christian cult as simply a continuation of the traditional one.

It has been seen, then, that the emotional character of Holy
Spirit church services often results in an outpouring of the Spirit,
either on the whole congregation or on individual members. This

is regarded as the most important part of worship because the Holy Spirit itself is believed to be present in the people in a trance and to speak through them. Possession makes a person gain recognition as a true member of the Church. It also releases tensions and thereby makes a person feel purified, and this appears to be an important reason why it has come to be regarded as desirable in a social situation with many tensions caused by great changes. Under these circumstances, spirit possession, as known traditionally in individual cases, has developed into a group cult which can give the benefits of this experience to a large number of people. And in the context of Christian worship the possessing spirit has come to be interpreted as the Holy Spirit.

Revelation and Interpretation of Dreams and Visions
Speaking in tongues is the most important way in which the Holy Spirit reveals itself to people during worship. But revelations that come at other times may be related at church services so that the whole congregation can know about them. This applies to revelations through dreams and visions.

Like speaking in tongues, dreams and visions may come to any Holy Spirit Church member, though some see more than others through these phenomena. The Church leaders hold that visions and dreams are basically the same kind of revelation, the only difference being that visions come to a person who is awake, and their contents are so clear that there is no need for interpretation, while dreams come to a person who is asleep, and their message is often brought in pictures, so interpretation is necessary before the Church can understand their significance (interviews with Japhet Zale Ambula, 2 May 1975, Kefa Ayub Mavuru, 10 June 1975, and Eliakim Keverenge Atonya, 27 June 1975).

In the early years, anyone who had had a dream or seen a vision would stand up in church and relate it to the rest of the congregation. Nowadays this happens less frequently. Only the Gospel Holy Spirit of East Africa has a regular practice of asking members to tell their dreams and visions. In the Lyahuka Church of East Africa and in the Holy Spirit Church of East Africa it happens sometimes, but I never saw it happen in the African Church of Holy Spirit. The practice of the Gospel Holy Spirit of East Africa in this respect, with people being urged by the leaders to stand up and relate what they have seen, probably reflects what

was done in all congregations some years back. Here more revelations seem to come through dreams than visions, possibly
because their rather mysterious content makes them appear more
important. After a hymn or two one of the leaders will stand up
and interpret the revelations brought by the Holy Spirit through
these dreams. There is often a rather detailed interpretation of the
first dream, with the comments on the others tending to suggest
that they reveal the same thing.

The reason why people in the other three Churches no longer
openly describe their dreams or visions is the same as it is for why
messages brought through speaking in tongues are no longer interpreted directly to the congregation. Church leaders now believe
that dreams and visions do not necessarily come from God. Satan
may deceive people through such phenomena and make them
believe that what he says is a revelation by the Holy Spirit. Therefore, instead of encouraging their members to announce their
revelations in front of everybody, they ask them to tell them to
their leaders, who will then look into whether the dreams or
visions are of significance for the Church (interviews with Japhet
Zale Ambula, 2 May 1975, Kefa Ayub Mavuru, 10 June 1975,
and Eliakim Keverenge Atonya, 27 June 1975).

However, despite the more cautious judgement of their source
of inspiration, dreams and visions are still regarded as important
phenomena in all the Holy Spirit Churches. This corresponds to
their importance in the traditional culture. Here too, not all
dreams were regarded as significant. Many were thought to bring
messages from the ancestors of whoever had seen them, just as
dreams in the Holy Spirit Churches are thought to bring messages
from God through the Holy Spirit. Traditionally, people simply
talked about their dreams; no expert was believed to possess the
ability to give authoritative interpretations (Wagner 1949: 210). In
the early days, by telling other members about their dreams or
visions, the Holy Spirit people were very likely following this
tradition. The discovery over the years that not everything
revealed in this way benefited the Church created a need for interpretation by a person who was thought to have a better understanding of the ways of the Spirit than ordinary members. This
caution has now been taken a step further in that dreams and
visions are mostly told privately to a leader, who also now interprets them without involving the whole congregation.

The services in the Holy Spirit Churches have therefore changed since the early days of the movement. Though the main aims of worship, to praise God and experience His presence, remain the same, a good deal of the original spontaneity has disappeared. Praise still plays an important role in worship, especially as expressed through singing hymns in a very lively manner and, though not necessarily at every meeting, through speaking in tongues. People praise God because He has given them the gift of salvation and of everything they need. But members of the congregation are also reminded of these gifts and are taught what is required of them before they can reach the final stage of salvation and go to heaven. The Church doctrines are taught through the same hymns through which the congregation praises God, and also through preaching and reciting psalms, which serve as confessions of faith in the main points of the Church's belief. Prayers are an important part of the service and, through them, God is asked to be near His people and to give them His blessings.

But the necessary condition for any communion with God and therefore for any meaningful church service is purity from all evil. At an early stage of the meeting demons have therefore to be driven out of the church, and everybody has to confess their sins and ask God for forgiveness. Praying, preaching and reciting psalms can only begin once these purification rituals have been carried out. Also, the highest form of communion with God, possession by the Holy Spirit, is only possible once the meeting has been purified and all sins been confessed. Only then is the way open for the Holy Spirit to descend upon the congregation, and such a state of possession does occur at many church services. The emotionalism of the singing, praying and preaching helps prepare the atmosphere for an outpouring of the Spirit, when people roll around on the floor and speak in tongues, their utterances regarded as the highest form of praise and prayer, a sign that God Himself is present through His Holy Spirit and is speaking through His people.

Possession was originally looked upon in this way, with people openly revealing the revelations they believed had been given to them through the Holy Spirit while they were speaking in tongues. Nowadays the Churches are more cautious. Experience has shown that such revelations do not always serve to build up the congregation, and the spontaneous recounting of them, as well as of those received through dreams and visions, has all but stopped. The Church leaders have to look at the content of the revelations to judge whether they are truly from the Holy Spirit.

The relatively fixed pattern followed during church services also reflects the disappearance of some of the original spontaneity. In theory the Spirit is still the true leader of the meeting and will lead it as it wishes. But in practice there are rules, developed over the years, that guide the conduct of meetings. Such rules make people feel secure — they know what is expected of them — and they limit the possibilities of the meeting turning against the principles of the Church.

The original spontaneity in worshipping God and receiving the Holy Spirit has therefore been limited over the years. But this has been done through a natural development of forms, and the pattern that has emerged should not be looked upon as restricting the freedom of the Spirit. The relatively fixed forms may be seen rather as a framework that enables the members of the Holy Spirit Churches to express their feelings towards God and to experience His presence, and to do this in ways that are meaningful and familiar to them.

3. The Role of the Holy Spirit Churches in the Lives of their Members

Frequent Church Services

In the Holy Spirit Churches there are normally four meetings a week — one on Tuesdays or Wednesdays, one on Fridays or Saturdays, and one on the Sabbath day (which is on Saturday in the Holy Spirit Church of East Africa and on Sunday in the other Churches) there are two meetings, one very early in the morning and one in the middle of the day (interviews with Peter Ihaji, 25 June 1975, Nathan Keya, 7 March 1975, Manoah Lumwagi, 24 June 1975, and Japhet Zale Ambula, 19 December 1974). One of the meetings in the middle of the week is theoretically supposed to be a women's meeting, but, according to Nathan Keya, if they have the courage, men can also go to it. Manoah Lumwagi says that women are responsible for organizing their own meetings, but that they may need advice from men and may ask men to preach and pray. So it looks as if, in practice, all the meetings are attended by both sexes. The reason for having so many meetings each week, according to Nathan Keya, is that many things happen during a week and it is therefore necessary to come together in the middle of the week to confess and to ask God for forgiveness. And there has to be a meeting on Fridays so that people can prepare themselves for the Sunday meetings.

As I mentioned earlier, there are also monthly, quarterly and yearly meetings. These are particularly festive occasions when members from different areas meet and worship together. Women also have their own monthly and quarterly meetings, and so do young people. All members are invited to attend any or all of these meetings, so there are numerous opportunities for worship.

It has been seen that the main aims of worship in the Holy

Spirit Churches are to praise God for the assurance of salvation He has given to His people and for all His blessings, and to experience His presence anew.

Because purity of heart is a necessary condition for any real communion with God, purification rites have to take place at the beginning of every meeting and these serve to relieve the members' stress. Any evil affecting them and causing bad feelings towards other people is driven away, and they become free to express their thankfulness and happiness by singing hymns, clapping and dancing. When the worship culminates in the outpouring of the Holy Spirit, further tensions are released as the worshippers give full vent to emotions normally kept under control by the demands of their everyday lives. The extreme emotionalism of the whole service, but particularly of receiving the Holy Spirit, allows Holy Spirit people to forget their problems, to be happy and to express themselves in emotionally satisfying ways.

Although confessing and receiving the Holy Spirit are basically individual experiences, the fact that everybody in the church follows the same pattern creates a fellowship between members. Through their experience of communion with God they also experience communion with each other, and this is of special importance in a society where traditional social relationships are rapidly breaking down.

Another important aspect of Holy Spirit church services is that nearly everybody is a leader of some kind. The organizational levels of village meetings, monthly meetings, quarterly meetings and yearly meetings provide many leadership opportunities. Although not all the Churches are as strictly organized as the African Church of Holy Spirit, they all have approximately the same leadership pattern. Each organizational level has a meeting leader, a secretary, a treasurer and a priest. These positions are held by men, except for one or two village leaders who are women. But in their parallel organization women hold corresponding leadership positions. There are also youth meetings leaders and prophets; the latter are sometimes appointed as priests, but may also stand apart from the normal leadership system. Besides these official leaders there are a number of minor leaders in each congregation. These include song leaders, of whom the majority are women, and drummers, who are mostly men (interview with Peter Ihaji, 25 June 1975).

Considering the relatively small number of members in each village congregation, nearly everyone holds one or another of these leadership positions. The amount of influence each individual can exercise in running the church and its services stands in sharp contrast to the opportunities available to exercise influence in the secular society. Here they hold no positions of importance and are often confined to being passive observers of what happens. But everybody has a chance to influence church activities and this gives them an important sense of their own worth.

The frequent church services in the Holy Spirit churches therefore serve to relieve the members of the strains of their everyday lives and to set them free to express their emotions and be happy. For them, this is equivalent to an experience of God as the one who drives away all evil and who is present with them through his Holy Spirit, and their happiness takes the form of praise to God. Every member takes an active part in the services for worship, and their experience of communion with God therefore at the same time becomes an experience of communion with their fellow church members. This feeling of fellowship between members is strengthened by nearly everybody being a leader and playing his or her part in running the meetings. In ordinary life these people often have to be passive onlookers to events that threaten their relations with other people. But in the meetings for worship in the Holy Spirit churches a fellowship is created within which each person is important as an active participator, and within which all are free to express themselves. Because of this important function of church services many members want to attend as often as possible, and this is probably why there are so many meetings.

Church Ceremonies at Crucial Stages of Life

Infancy

In traditional Abaluyia culture, each stage of the life of an individual was marked with special ceremonies that established his or her position in society. There were ceremonies to mark the stages of birth, adolescence, marriage and death. The Friends Church, like other Churches, also has ceremonies that indicate the transition from one of these stages to another. It is therefore natural that in the Holy Spirit Churches similar ceremonies are found which show the care of the Church for each individual member.

Whenever a child is born into one of the Holy Spirit Churches, a priest prays for it. In the Holy Spirit Church of East Africa the mother brings the child to the church, while in the other three Churches the priest goes to the child's home to pray for it there (interviews with Japhet Zale Ambula, 27 January 1975, Timotheo Hezekiah Shitsimi, 6 June 1976, Jotham Eshera, 29 April 1975, and Timona Luvai Malao, 6 April 1975). The child is given a card to prove that it is now accepted by the Church. There is no water baptism, and in this the Holy Spirit Churches follow the example of the Friends, who regard water baptism as unbiblical because Matthew 3:11 and John 1:33 show that while John was baptized with water, the baptism of Jesus was with the Holy Spirit (interviews with Charles Wakhisi, 24 January 1975, and Japhet Zale Ambula, 13 January 1975).

If the child is a boy he will be prayed for when he is eight days old. If it is a girl this will happen when she is two weeks old. This rule is not taken over from the Friends Church, but has been found in Leviticus 12, which says that if a woman has given birth to a boy she shall be unclean for seven days and on the eighth day he shall be circumcised. If she has given birth to a girl she shall be unclean for two weeks. The explanation for why this rule has been felt to be relevant to members of the Holy Spirit Churches is probably because a similar period of uncleanness was observed in these peoples' traditional culture. Here the period was two days if the child was a girl and three days if it was a boy (Wagner 1949: 302). But in the Churches the traditional notion has been given a biblical interpretation.

Traditionally, when a baby was two or three months old a sacrifice was performed to ensure the spirits' benevolence towards it (Wagner 1949: 311). In the Holy Spirit Churches this ceremony is combined with the observation of a period of uncleanliness, prescribed in Leviticus 12, after which the priest prays for God's blessings over the child. Another traditional ceremony, the naming ceremony (Wagner 1949: 313), has also been combined with the blessing ceremony. This is when, as in the Friends Church, the child is given a Christian name.

Adolescence
Traditionally, on reaching adolescence boys are circumcised and this custom is still upheld by all Abaluyia people. But the Church

has become actively involved in the ceremony for children in the Holy Spirit Churches. The operation itself is still performed by the same circumciser who operates on boys who do not belong to these Churches. But on the evening before the circumcision the boys of the Church gather in one house, and here they spend the night together with a priest. They confess their sins, and the priest prays for them. This may parallel the traditional confession reported by Wagner from among the Tiriki (Wagner 1949: 344), but it is also a natural action in the Holy Spirit Churches where evil spirits are believed to be an ever-present danger. After the operation comes the period of healing, and here the Church rule is adhered to that no use of medicine, whether traditional or modern, is allowed. At the 'coming out' ceremony after the period of healing (Wagner 1949: 363), the Church is again involved, in that the elders come and admonish the boys to follow the Church rules in their adult lives (interview with Timotheo Hezekiah Shitsimi, 6 June 1976).

But apart from this Church adaptation of a traditional ceremony, the Holy Spirit Church of East Africa and the Lyahuka Church of East Africa also have a special church ceremony for adolescent boys and girls. They go through a period of learning of about three weeks, after which there is a ceremony in the church at which they are accepted into full membership and given a second card, different from the one they were given as infants. What they learn during the three weeks amounts to a few important Bible passages such as Psalms 1 and 23 and John 3:16, and they are taught by the Church elders how to confess their sins in the right way so that they may receive the Holy Spirit (interviews with Japhet Zale Ambula, 27 January 1975, and Jotham Eshera, 29 April 1975).

The system of having different cards for children and for adults is taken over from the Friends Church, and so is the period of learning and the subsequent ceremony in the church. But the Holy Spirit Churches have simplified the procedure for becoming a full member. In the Friends Church there were two cards, an associate membership card and a full membership card, besides the card given to children. And before becoming an associate member, as well as before becoming a full member, there were periods of learning that lasted for several months. The African Church of Holy Spirit has simplified even further. Here there is no official period of learning, nor is there a special ceremony in the church when the young people receive their adult membership cards. They are simply given the cards when they are considered old enough to become full members (interviews with Peter Ihaji, 25 June 1975, and Kefa Ayub Mavuru, 9 March 1976).

Marriage

At the time of a marriage the Holy Spirit Churches are again involved in the transition of the individuals involved to a new stage of life. The African Church of Holy Spirit, the Holy Spirit Church of East Africa and the Lyahuka Church of East Africa all have the right to register marriages according to Kenya government law (interviews with Timotheo Hezekiah Shitsimi, 6 June 1976, Japhet Zale Ambula, 15 March 1976, and Jotham Eshera, 29 April 1975). The Church is involved in the preparations for the marriage in that communications are set up between the boy's and girl's respective village meetings and the Church elders act as intermediaries between the two families. At one time the Churches were more involved at this stage than they are now. At least in the African Church of Holy Spirit, which seems to have been the strictest on this point, a boy and girl were not allowed to choose whom they wanted to marry. The Church made the decision for them. This was done by asking people in the church whether anybody had received a prophecy or dream about who was to become the wife of a certain boy. Once a girl had been found in this way, she would be told about it, and since the choice was considered to have been made by the Holy Spirit, the young people normally followed it. This is still considered an ideal way of choosing a marriage partner. But in actual practice there is much more freedom nowadays for young people to choose whom they want to marry, and in fact the majority of marriages are now by elopement, as they are outside these Churches.

Because the constitutions of the Holy Spirit Churches only recognize registered marriages, young couples who have eloped come to the church later on to be officially married by the priest, who is authorized to act as a registrar of marriages. The Church, however, disapproves of this kind of marriage, which it regards as 'temporary', as opposed to the 'honourable' marriage of a couple who have not eloped first (interview with Timotheo Hezekiah Shitsimi, 6 June 1976).

The wedding ceremony itself differs little from those of other Churches. The main part of the celebration takes place at the bridegroom's home, which is the tradition among Abaluyia people.

Death

Finally, like the Friends and other Churches, the Holy Spirit Churches are involved in the funerals of members who die. Important elements of this ceremony are driving away evil spirits and praying for God's blessing of the dead person (*Mpango wa Mazishi* n.d.). Traditionally, a so-called hair-shaving ceremony was held on the third day after a funeral, when those who had been in close contact with the deceased shortly before his or her death would shave their heads as a form of ritual purification. At this ceremony the distribution of the dead person's property would be decided upon and people would discuss the cause of death (Wagner 1949: 485). The Holy Spirit Churches also have a ceremony on the third day after burial. But in these Churches it is interpreted as a celebration of the resurrection of the deceased, a parallel to the resurrection of Jesus on the third day after his burial. Singing resurrection hymns and reading scriptures relating to resurrection, for instance 1. Corinthians 15:20–2, are important elements of this ceremony (*Mpango wa Mazishi* n.d.; interview with Japhet Zale Ambula, 19 December 1974).

But the most important ceremony held for the person who has died, at least in the African Church of Holy Spirit, is the memorial meeting 40 days after burial. Just as Jesus ascended to heaven 40 days after his resurrection, according to Acts 1:1–11, so the dead person is thought to go to heaven on that day if he or she has been a faithful Christian. A meeting attended by many people, both members and non-members, is held and there is much singing and joy to celebrate the dead person's final salvation in heaven. Preaching on the theme of judgement reminds those present that if they follow the ways of God they too will go to heaven on the fortieth day after their funeral, but that if they do not they will go to hell (*Mpango wa Mazishi* n.d.; interview with Timotheo Hezekiah Shitsimi, 6 June 1976; attendance at memorial meeting of the African Church of Holy Spirit at Mukomari, Isukha, 1 February 1976).

This ceremony does not exist in the Friends Church. Traditionally, the first animal sacrifice was offered to the spirit of the deceased about three months after death, and the significance of this sacrifice, according to Wagner (1949: 501), is that it establishes the dead person's social status in the spirit world. The African Church of Holy Spirit memorial service corresponds closely to the traditional ceremony in that the dead person's status in heaven is thought to become established on this occasion.

The Holy Spirit Churches demonstrate their care for each individual member by performing ceremonies at the crucial points when a person passes from one stage of life to another. Such ceremonies were also performed in these people's traditional culture, as well as in the Friends Church, and they are therefore not a feature of the Holy Spirit Churches alone. But the way in which the Holy Spirit Churches perform these ceremonies shows a closer adaptation of traditional ceremonies to Christian practices than in the Friends Church, where the ceremonies were performed without much regard for what used to happen traditionally. Through this adaptation the Holy Spirit Churches incorporate their members' traditional ceremonies into Christian worship. They integrate traditional and Christian forms into a whole, so that no aspect of the lives of their members is left out of the care of the Church.

Prayers for the Problems of Individuals

Curative and Preventive 'Medicine'
It has been seen above that in the Holy Spirit Church of East Africa there are at each church service prayers for the specific problems of each individual member — prayers for healing, for success at school, for women to bear children. Though prayers of this kind are less common at the other Holy Spirit Churches' meetings for worship, they are nevertheless important. The only difference is that these prayers are normally said on other occasions.

In all the Holy Spirit Churches it is common practise for priests or village leaders to go to people's homes to pray whenever they are asked to do so. Members ask their leaders to come and pray for them for many different reasons. There may be disease in the home, quarrelling between husband and wife, or a person may have committed a sin and wants the elder to drive away the demons that caused the wrongdoing (interviews with Manoah

Lumwagi, 13 April 1975 and Timotheo Hezekiah Shitsimi, 6 June 1976; information from Petro Sida, 15 June 1975). .

In all such cases, the elder goes to the home to which he has been called, and here he first of all asks the person or persons concerned to confess all their sins. When they have confessed, he drives away the demons with shouts of '*gi twulidzwe*', prays for God to forgive them for all their sins and then prays for the specific problem. Since disease and all other evils are seen to be caused by demons, the procedure is the same in all cases. If people are sick, the elder lays his hands on them while praying that they may become well, but no material objects are used to promote recovery. Prayer is the only 'medicine' allowed in the Holy Spirit Churches (interview with Timotheo Hezekiah Shitsimi, 6 June 1976).

When an elder goes to people's homes to pray for special problems as described above, it is 'medicine' for healing. But there is also 'medicine' for prevention. A priest or village leader may receive a message through a dream or prophecy to go to the home of a certain member to pray to prevent some misfortune, for instance disease to humans or animals (interview with Timotheo Hezekiah Shitsimi, 6 June 1976). This corresponds to Wagner's distinction between two kinds of measures that could be taken in traditional Abaluyia society against evil powers threatening human beings. He says that traditionally the Abaluyia people employed one set of measures to protect themselves against an evil power exercising its influence over a person, and another set of measures to drive the evil away once misfortune had struck (Wagner 1949: 178).

Church Discipline
The care church elders show for each individual member through prayers in their homes is also shown, though indirectly, through church discipline. The Holy Spirit Churches have set up certain rules which members have to follow. It is forbidden to drink, smoke and dance. Polygamy is not allowed for those who are already members, but non-members who are already married to more than one wife may be accepted into membership.[1]

---

1. In the constitutions of the Holy Spirit Church of East Africa, the Lyahuka Church of East Africa and the Gospel Holy Spirit of East Africa.

Ane Marie Bak Rasmussen, the author.

Facing Page, top. dr. theol. Anna Marie Aagaard and Ane Marie Bak Rasmussen (Konsulent Kt), at the Danish Church Days, 2-7 July 1983.

Middle. The family in Aarhus, 1 January 1991; Zakarias, Joseph Wasike Mululu, Ane Marie and Hans Peter.

Bottom. A gift of the cross to the author from Timotheo Hezekiah Shitsimi, High Priest of the African Church of Holy Spirit at his home Dumbeni, Kabras, 14 December 1987.

This page, above. Memorial to the author.

Below. The author and Kenyan Ambassador J. Wanyoike and his wife Janet, Aarhus 4 June 1980.

Above. Old and new churches at Lugala headquarters, Isukha.

Below. The late Roda and Zakaria Kwanusu Mululu, Makhonge Friends Church, Chwele, pioneer members among Elgon Friends, Bungoma.

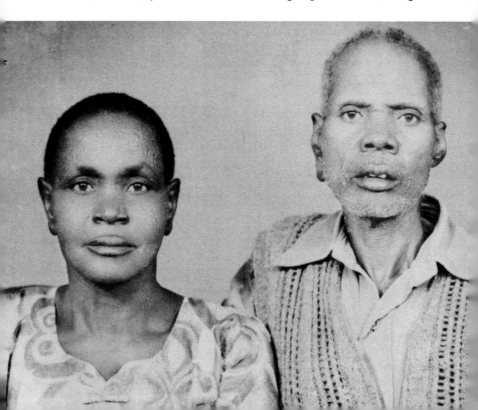

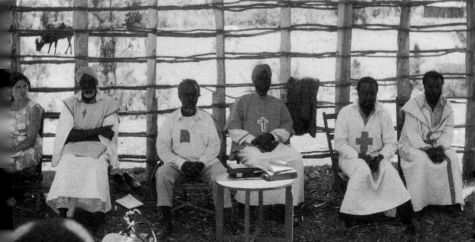

This page, above. Enis Kadali, founder of Gospel Holy Spirit of East Africa, leading church service at Endeli headquarters, 6 April 1975.

Below. Some members still have long hair as all of the Holy Spirit people had during the early days.

Previous page, top. Mrs and Petro Tsimajero, pioneer members, who was High Priest after Kefa Ayubu Mavuru, of the African Church of Holy Spirit at Lugala, Isukha, until his death.

Middle. Leaders of the Lyahuka Church of East Africa and the author, at Lukuvuli, North Maragoli.

Bottom. The author and leaders in Endeli Church of Gospel Holy Spirit of East Africa.

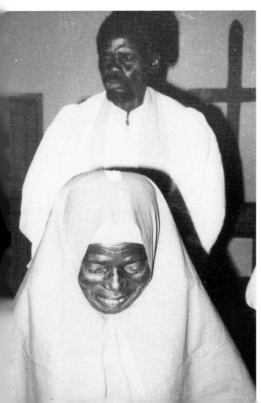

This page, left. Turbans, beards and crosses are some of the characteristics of the Holy Spirit people.

Below. An old prophetess in the church.

Next page, top. Prayer for sadaka, the money collected in church. (By Japhet Zale-Ambula who was Archbishop of Holy Spirit Church of East Africa until his death at Bukoyani headquarters, South Maragoli).

Middle. Confession at church service at Lugala headquarters of the African Church of Holy Spirit, 20 March 1975.

Bottom. At the outdoor meeting, people form a circle with their flags in the middle, and here they hold a service for worship. (Lyahuka Church of East Africa at Chavakali, North Maragoli, 4 January 1975).

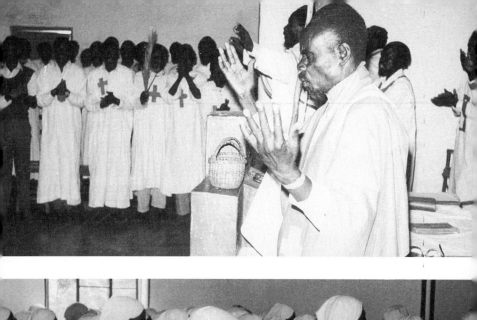

These rules are not very different from those found in the Friends Church. Very serious sins are adultery, stealing, killing and robbery, and so is marrying by elopement without the permission of the Church.

If a member commits one of these serious sins, his or her membership of the Church is suspended for a period of time. The reason for this, according to Timotheo Hezekiah Shitsimi, is that it is necessary to punish such people so that they learn to fear the punishment God will give them if they do not stop their bad ways. Also, if they remain in the Church they would defile it, in that other members might learn from their bad example.

The period such people have to spend outside the Church is not fixed. It depends on the attitude of the sinner. It may be three weeks, it may be a month, or perhaps three months. But if they are repentant, the period is not be very long. Their reacceptance into the Church takes place when the Church elders have been told by God through a dream or prophecy that the time has come for the person in question to confess in front of the congregation. They then attend a church meeting, where everybody listens as they openly confess to whatever sin they have committed. After that they pray to Jesus for forgiveness, saying, 'Yesu yasamehe', and the congregation helps them by answering, 'Yesu akhusamehe'.[2]

Only if the sin is serious and all the members know about it will the person in question be barred from the Church for some time. If the offence is of a less serious nature and only the Church elders know about it, the confession is made to the elders in the privacy of the sinner's own home, but in the same manner as described above (interview with Timotheo Hezekiah Shitsimi, 6 June 1976).

Both the serious Church discipline, which suspends a person's membership for a period of time, and the more lenient type, which only involves the Church elders, serve to impress the rules and teachings of the Church upon its members. Such rules help to preserve the unity of the Church. On the one hand they make the members recognizable to each other and, on the other, they mark them off as a group that stands apart from the surrounding world. The rules that guide the conduct of Church members, as well as those that prescribe a certain kind of dress, such as turbans and

2. This means, respectively, 'Jesus, forgive me' and 'May Jesus forgive you'.

red crosses, therefore create a fellowship between members which
has been compared with the traditional fellowship of the clan or
tribe, which was also in many cases guarded by certain rules, such
as those about the observance of taboos and about circumcision
(Welbourn and Ogot 1966: 141).

In this close fellowship in the Holy Spirit Churches it is
important for each member to obey the Church's rules so that its
unity is not broken. Welbourn and Ogot's comparison of independent Churches with traditional clans is limited by the fact that
Church fellowship is based on free choice, while in the clan it was
based on biological inheritance. And this difference makes the
observance of the rules of the fellowship even more important. If
members break those rules, it not only sets them apart from the
accepted norms of the fellowship, but, unless steps are taken to
punish the offender so that these norms are upheld, threatens the
unity for the rest of the members.

Church discipline and the elders' prayers for their members'
problems are thus reflections of the closely-knit fellowship that
exists in the Holy Spirit Churches. They also demonstrate the
Churches' double concern, namely for both the fellowship as such
and for each individual member. Those who belong to this fellowship are cared for by their Church elders, who come to their
homes to pray for whatever problems they might have. The
security of the traditional clan community, with its close fellowship between the members of the clan, has therefore been
recreated in the Holy Spirit Churches where no member is left out
in the cold, but where all members care for the welfare of the
others, and where the unity of the Church is closely guarded and
offenders against it are punished.

Cooperation among Members for Practical Purposes
It has already been seen above that the Holy Spirit Churches care
not only for the spiritual welfare of their members but for all
aspects of their lives. The Churches' concern for the material
aspects of life is exemplified in the cooperation that takes place
among members for practical purposes. This especially happens
among the women, and the most common form of cooperation is
the formation of work groups. The women in such a group may
work in turn in each other's fields. They may also work for other
members of the same Church and thereby earn some money. And

they can even do farm work for non-members, in which case they charge more than they would from a member (interview with Manoah Lumwagi, 24 June 1975; information from Timotheo Hezekiah Shitsimi, 28 March 1975, and from church service at Bukoyani headquarters of the Holy Spirit Church of East Africa, 18 January 1975). Money collected in this manner benefits the members of the Church in various ways. Some women's groups give a certain amount to each woman in turn at regular intervals, but the most common practice is to save it in case of difficulties among members of the congregation. Large amounts are especially needed if someone dies. In that case, the members of the Church contribute money to those left behind. The money collected by women's work groups is often used in such cases, but a special fund-raising may also be arranged to collect enough to cover all the expenses of a funeral (memorial service at Mukomari, Isukha, of the African Church of Holy Spirit, 1 February 1975).

The reason why women are so active in work groups is, according to Manoah Lumwagi, that many husbands are away from home, working in other areas of the country. Because of this the women need whatever support they can get from each other to carry the responsibility for their homes and families. Perhaps because they feel a special need for the fellowship provided by the Church, women are normally very active members. If a member becomes sick, or other difficulties arise in someone's home, the women often go there and help in many practical ways.

Formally, there may not be much difference between the Holy Spirit Churches and the Friends Church in the various matters discussed in this chapter. Originally, the Friends also held several church services a week, though now they usually have only one or two. The Friends Church also performs ceremonies for an individual member who passes into a new stage of life. Friends pastors may also visit members in their homes and pray for them, and women's work groups and other forms of cooperation among members exist in other Churches as well. The difference lies more in the way in which many of these things are done. It has been seen how the meetings for worship in the Holy Spirit Churches developed in such a way as to satisfy the needs of the members. When discussing the ceremonies performed for individuals at birth, adolescence and death, I pointed out how the Holy Spirit Churches incorporated far more traditional notions into their ceremonies than they did in the Friends Church, thereby integrating the religious thoughts of their members into a whole. Welbourn has pointed out that as mission Churches increase their membership they easily develop into large, impersonal institutions no longer able to create an effective fellowship to reach into all the areas of their members' lives. But many people feel the need for such fellowship because of the insecurity they experience in a rapidly changing society. It is provided by the independent Churches, in this case by the Holy Spirit Churches. With their small congregations and the active involvement of all members in the running of the Church, they are able to realize the fellowship which has largely ceased to exist in the mission Churches (Welbourn 1961: 202).

4. Strengthening and Extending the Work of the Holy Spirit Churches

Special Prayers for the Church

Lilinda Meetings

The meetings for worship in the Holy Spirit Churches have, as seen above, been brought into relatively fixed patterns. The original freedom of every member to do as he felt led by the Holy Spirit has to a large extent disappeared. It has been replaced by forms which ensure that what is done at church services conforms to the true aims of the Churches and that members feel at home at meetings that follow familiar patterns.

But about three or four times a year special meetings are held in these churches which have a closer resemblance to the meetings held during the early days of the Holy Spirit movement. They are called 'lilinda' meetings, 'waiting' meetings. The intention with them is that members shall be together for a number of days and 'wait' for the Holy Spirit to descend upon them. They are renewal meetings at which the Holy Spirit people seek to revive the spirit of the early days when they thought of nothing but confessing, praying, praising God and receiving the Holy Spirit (interviews with Japhet Zale Ambula, 13 January 1975, Timotheo Hezekiah Shitsimi, 3 June 1976, and Manoah Lumwagi, 23 June 1975).

These meetings are supposed to be held four times a year in the Holy Spirit Church of East Africa and three times a year in the African Church of Holy Spirit. But in the latter Church, at least, this rule is not followed strictly (interview with Peter Ihaji, 25 June 1975), and the actual practice seems to be that local congregations or monthly meetings hold lilinda meetings when they feel the need for it. Members come together at one place and stay there for a number of days, leaving all their everyday worries behind. Leaders instruct the ordinary members in the proper ways to confess their sins. Everybody confesses and prays for God's presence among them, there is an outpouring of the Holy Spirit on young and old, on leaders and ordinary members alike, and people sing hymns of praise to God for His Spirit which He has given to them.

The members of the Holy Spirit Churches are strengthened in their faith during these *lilinda* meetings through repeated experiences of being purified and of encountering God's presence through the Holy Spirit. They are all reassured that they belong to God's chosen people. Just as the shared experience of receiving the Holy Spirit at ordinary church services creates a fellowship among those present, so it happens to an even greater extent at these meetings, where the experience is repeated for days on end. Thus, though the purpose of *lilinda* meetings is primarily to renew every single member's faith, they also serve another important function, namely of strengthening the fellowship among all Church members and collectively giving them the assurance that they are indeed God's chosen people.

Mountain Prayer

The most important kind of prayer in the Holy Spirit Churches is prayer at a mountain (interviews with Timotheo Hezekiah Shitsimi, 6 June 1976, and Kefa Ayub Mavuru, 9 March 1976; information about church service at Bukoyani headquarters of Holy Spirit Church of East Africa, 6 July 1975; visit to Maragoli Hill with Petro Sida and Zebedaioh Malolo of the Gospel Holy Spirit of East Africa, 14 June 1975). There is no specific mountain to which all of them go, but in each area there is one they normally choose for their prayers. The Holy Spirit may direct them to a different mountain, in which case they follow its command. Likewise, they never go to a mountain for just ordinary prayers, but only when the Holy Spirit has shown them they must go there to pray very seriously, and it normally happens only once or twice a year. Not all members may pray at the mountains, only the top leaders of each Church.

According to Timotheo Hezekiah Shitsimi, prayers offered at a mountain are for very serious problems that affect the whole Church, the whole country or even the world. Leaders may be shown by the Holy Spirit that they have to go to a mountain to pray to prevent great catastrophes from happening, or they may be commanded to go there after some grave event has occurred, such as the start of an epidemic or famine, or even a war. And when they pray at a mountain they always expect God to answer their prayers.

His explanation of why it is necessary to go to a mountain for such important prayers is that a mountain is a quiet place. Here the leaders are able to concentrate on their prayers for as long as the Holy Spirit shows them they must stay there, often two or three days. Many members of the Holy Spirit Churches undoubtedly feel there are reasons for going to a mountain other than simply that it is a quiet place. Zebedaioh Malolo says that God himself lives in the mountains, and he is therefore closer to human beings there than anywhere else. Petro Sida and Kefa Ayub Mavuru both say that when Church leaders pray at a mountain they receive many revelations from God, more than at any other place. There seems to be, therefore, a feeling among members of these Churches that mountains are the most sacred of all places, and this is why only selected persons can go there and why the prayers offered there must be of special importance.

Both Turner (1967b: 221) and Sundkler (1970: 198) point out the important role holy mountains play for most African independent Churches, and see this as paralleling the significance attached to mountains in the traditional religions of Africa. In the case of the Holy Spirit Churches a similar parallel can be drawn with the traditional religion of the Abaluyia people. Wagner (1949: 290) mentions the half-yearly sacrifice performed among the Logoli people on a mountain in south Maragoli. This was the only sacrifice on a tribal scale performed among the Abaluyia, and the objective was to secure a good harvest, or at least to prevent a harvest failure. It was imperative that this most important sacrifice had to be performed on a specific mountain, and only two persons, the sacrificial priests, were allowed to go all the way up to the sacred grove.

The parallels with the mountain prayers of the Holy Spirit Churches can be clearly seen. Here also, only top leaders are allowed to go to the holy place for this most important prayer. They go only rarely and when they do it is to offer prayers for very important problems that affect the whole Church, the whole country or the whole world, just as the yield of the harvest was of vital importance to the whole of the Logoli people, and sacrifices had to be offered to secure its success.

Prayers at the Grave of Jacob Buluku

The Holy Spirit Church of East Africa holds special prayers for strengthening the Church which are not found in the other Holy Spirit Churches. These are said once a year at the grave of Jacob Buluku. On 15 March each year members of the Church gather at his grave for a memorial meeting to celebrate the anniversary of his death, which occurred on that date in 1938. A meeting for worship is held in the style of other church services, and the prayers during this meeting concentrate especially on asking God to let the members of the Church stand firm in their faith, just as Jacob Buluku did, even in the face of severe persecution (interview with Japhet Zale Ambula, 19 December 1974; attendance at memorial meeting for Jacob Buluku at his grave at Bukoyani headquarters of the Holy Spirit Church of East Africa, 15 March 1976).

Some members appear to believe that the purpose of the meeting is to pray to Jacob Buluku, who is now in heaven and can therefore be regarded as an intermediary between human beings and God. At the memorial meeting I attended, Japhet Zale Ambula warned several times against this tendency, emphasizing that Jacob Buluku was a human being and that he would therefore have nothing to give to other people if they tried to pray to him. The reason for the meeting, he said, was to remember Jacob, 'the lion', who remained faithful to the Holy Spirit movement despite persecution, and to urge members to follow his example and to pray to God for the strength to do so.

The Holy Spirit Churches therefore have special prayers that are seen to be of importance for the Church as a whole. Through the *lilinda* meetings for confession, prayer and receiving the Holy Spirit, not only the individual, but the whole fellowship of the Church, is strengthened. And, through the most important of all prayers, those offered on a mountain, the Church leaders ask God for the protection and deliverance from evil of the whole Church, as well as of all human beings.

The Search for Recognition by the Outside World

Lilinda meetings, mountain prayers and the prayers said at Jacob

Buluku's grave all serve to strengthen the inner life of the Holy Spirit Churches. Through these prayers the faith of individual members is renewed, and so is the fellowship between them. But the Holy Spirit Churches also attempt to gain strength through recognition by the outside world.

One way to gain this recognition is to seek connections with councils of Christian Churches. The African Church of Holy Spirit has for a number of years been a member of the National Christian Council of Kenya (Mavuru and Ihaji 1975), and at the general assembly of the World Council of Churches held in Nairobi in 1975 it was accepted into associate membership of this world body of Christian Churches (interview with Peter Ihaji, 1 February 1976).

The Lyahuka Church of East Africa has connections with the East Africa Christian Alliance and with the International Council of Christian Churches (information from Manoah Lumwagi, 12 February 1975), although, according to the *Kenya Churches Handbook*, it is not formally a member of any of these church bodies (Barrett et al. 1973: 186). The recognition gained through such relations with wider associations of churches is important for the prestige of the Holy Spirit Churches in the eyes of members, as well as in the eyes of other people. But it is not suggested that the wish for prestige is the only factor that leads them to seek such connections. The isolationist attitude of the early years has now all but disappeared, and they have come to realize the value of cooperation among different Churches. This change of attitude is also reflected in the fact that both the African Church of Holy Spirit and the Holy Spirit Church of East Africa have sent students for theological training to St Paul's United Theological College in Limuru (Barrett et al. 1973: 231, 244).

There are also attempts at cooperation between these Churches and other denominations at a less formal level. They have friendly relationships with most other Churches, and especially with the Friends Church and with the Pentecostal Assemblies of God, as well as with a number of other African independent Churches, for instance the African Israel Church Nineveh (interviews with Japhet Zale Ambula, 19 December 1974, and Eliakim Keverenge Atonya, 3 January 1975). An example of this is that whenever there is an important occasion, the African Church of Holy Spirit invites leaders of other Churches to attend, such as when a new quarterly meeting was opened in Tiriki location during Christmas 1974, and when a new church building was officially opened at the Lugala headquarters in April 1975.

On such occasions not only the leaders of other Churches are invited, but government officials and politicians as well. This reflects the change of attitude that has occurred over the years. While the Holy Spirit movement was originally isolationist and wanted to have as little as possible to do with the government, it is now positive towards the independent Kenya government and eager for its activities to be recognized by it. The same attitude is seen in that leaders urge their members to take part in development projects, and the leaders attend meetings called by local government officials and report back to the congregations what has taken place (meeting of the Holy Spirit Church of East Africa at Bukoyani headquarters, 6 July 1975; information from Japhet Zale Ambula, 15 March 1976). The isolationist attitude of the early years has therefore been given up, and the Holy Spirit Churches are now eager to receive recognition from the outside world, both from other Churches and from the government. Such recognition strengthens the position of the Churches in the eyes of other people and gives the members pride in their Church. But the Holy Spirit Churches do not only seek prestige. Members are urged to play an active role in the society around them by cooperating with other Churches and participating in government projects. The Churches are therefore trying to establish a position for themselves in society through active participation in its activities, and they try to do this without losing their own essential characteristics.

Outdoor Meetings and Processions

The Holy Spirit Churches show their special characteristics to the outside world when they have outdoor meetings, or when they march in processions along the roads. These processions usually occur when a big meeting, a monthly or quarterly meeting, is going to take place. Members from one village meeting then normally come to the meeting together, marching and singing and drumming, with the flag of the village church carried at the front of the procession.

Marching along the road in this way serves to strengthen the members' identification with their Church. They become keenly aware of belonging to a particular Church, symbolized by a flag carrying the Church's colours with the name of their village sewn onto it. The flag of the Holy Spirit Church of East Africa is red on the upper half and green on the lower, with the name of the church and of the particular village sewn in white. The flags of the other Holy Spirit Churches have white letters and crosses on a red background, and in the Lyahuka Church of East Africa the cross is enclosed in a circle, just as it is on the clothes of its members. But processions not only serve to give the members a strong feeling of identification with their Church. They are also a means of evangelization. When they drum, sing and show their happiness, Holy Spirit people bear witness to their faith towards the non-members who see them.

Processions may also be formed by a smaller number of people, no more than ten or twelve, for the direct purpose of evangelization. They march along the roads in the way described above and, when they feel the Holy Spirit direct them to do so, turn off the road and go to someone's house. Here they sing and preach, witnessing to their faith, and if the members of the family they happen to visit are interested in their message, they normally stay there and continue their witnessing until the following day (interview with Timotheo Hezekiah Shitsimi, 6 June 1976).

Outdoor meetings are another form of evangelization. These are held in public places, often in market places. When felt directed by the Holy Spirit to hold a meeting of this kind, the people of the church come in procession to an appointed place where they form a circle with their flags planted in the middle. They now hold a meeting for worship for everybody to see, concentrating mainly on singing and preaching, often testifying to the forgiveness from sins they have found through their Holy Spirit church (attendance at outdoor meeting of the Lyahuka Church of East Africa at Chevakali, North Maragoli, 4 January 1975; interviews with Japhet Zale Ambula, 13 January 1975, and Timotheo Hezekiah Shitsimi, 6 June 1976). Though evangelization is the main aim of these outdoor meetings, they, like the other examples mentioned here, serve a double purpose — they also help strengthen the faith of the Holy Spirit people themselves and increase their sense of belonging to a particular church.

It has been seen, then, that the Holy Spirit Churches have various ways of strengthening their members' faith and the fellowship between them. The inner life of the Churches may be strengthened through *lilinda* meetings, or mountain prayer, or, in the case of the Holy Spirit Church of East Africa, through the prayers offered once a year at Jacob Buluku's graveside. Outwardly, these Churches are strengthened by the increased recognition they receive from other Churches, formally in Christian councils and informally through cooperation at the local level. They also gain outward strength from the recognition of the government, with which they try to maintain a good relationship. Through such recognition by non-members, the Holy Spirit Churches gain prestige, and this in turn strengthens their members' belief in the importance of their Church. This self-confidence finds expression in their wish to gain more members, and they carry out their evangelizing mission through outdoor meetings in public places and group visits to private homes, where they bear witness to their faith before potential new members. Processions along roads are another, more indirect, way of carrying out evangelization. But all these ways in which the Holy Spirit people bring their message to other people serve at the same time to strengthen their own sense of identification with their Church and their feeling of belonging to a fellowship, which is important in the society in which they live.

5. Beliefs of the Holy Spirit Churches

The Doctrine of the Holy Spirit

Speaking in Tongues
The Holy Spirit Churches were brought into existence because of the controversy with the Friends Africa Mission over the question of baptism with the Holy Spirit. Other factors may have contributed to the split in the years after 1927, but the fundamental theological difference between them, and the one which caused the separation, was in their attitudes to the manifestations of the Holy Spirit. For the Holy Spirit people, the experience of becoming possessed by the Spirit, during which they spoke in tongues and experienced other ecstatic phenomena, became the central point in their religious life. The Friends, on the other hand, while believing in the importance of the Holy Spirit, refused to recognize such phenomena as true manifestations of its presence.

Through the years the Holy Spirit people have held on to the belief in the validity of their original experience. Entering a trance and speaking in tongues, as well as such phenomena as dreams, visions and prophecy, are still regarded as the means through which the Holy Spirit communicates with human beings. Certain forms have developed along the way which bring the expressions of the presence of the Holy Spirit into recognizable patterns. Some leaders have become more cautious than they originally were and do not in all cases interpret these phenomena as true expressions of the Holy Spirit. But fundamentally, the attitude within these Churches to what is regarded as manifestations of the Holy Spirit has not changed. It is still thought to be desirable for every member to receive the Spirit, and if this has not happened after a number of years of membership it is regarded as proof that this person has not truly confessed all his or her sins (interview with

Timotheo Hezekiah Shitsimi, 3 June 1976). Therefore, every genuine Christian must at one time or another experience the baptism with the Holy Spirit.

The unmistakable sign that a person has received the Holy Spirit is that he or she enters a trance, rolls around on the floor and speaks in tongues. Timotheo Hezekiah Shitsimi says that in some cases people may be baptized with the Spirit and yet not speak in tongues. Their baptism will then be revealed in other ways, for instance through an ability to heal the sick. But generally speaking, a person can judge whether or not others have received the Spirit by seeing if they are able to speak in tongues.

When asked about the nature of speaking in tongues, what it really means, the Holy Spirit people give various answers. Many answer that people who speak in tongues are able to speak a language they ordinarily do not know (interviews with Kefa Ayub Mavuru, 10 June 1975, and Eliakim Keverenge Atonya, 27 June 1975). This is seen to parallel the day of Pentecost as described in Acts 2:1–4, when the disciples received the power to speak in different languages. English and Arabic are the two languages normally mentioned as being spoken in tongues. In fact, when people speak in tongues they often try to bring in English words they know, but never in a coherent way that could be described as speaking English. The difference here, compared with the day of Pentecost, is that, according to Acts 2, on that day the languages the disciples spoke served to bring the gospel to people of countries whose languages they did not know. In the Holy Spirit Churches there is no suggestion of the different languages members claim to speak serving a missionary purpose. Rather, the ability to speak them is regarded as mysterious, as proof of the extraordinary power given to them by the Holy Spirit.

Another interpretation of speaking in tongues is that it is a kind of prayer (interviews with Eliakim Keverenge Atonya, 27 June 1975, and Timotheo Hezekiah Shitsimi, 3 June 1976). Timotheo Hezekiah Shitsimi gave as an example the use of tongues at a Good Friday church service I attended at his church at Dumbeni in South Kabras location on 28 March 1975. This meeting lasted for several hours, but for the last hour or so, every member of the Church was rolling on the floor, crying and shouting and speaking in tongues. This outburst of emotion was sparked off by a long sermon preached by Timotheo Hezekiah Shitsimi himself, in which he related in great detail what the gospels tell us about the death of Jesus. When, towards the end, he stressed that Jesus died because of the sins of people, including those present here, and that they had to repent all their sins if they wished to be saved, this was the decisive point at which everybody suddenly fell to the ground and began to cry in the Spirit. Timotheo Hezekiah Shitsimi claims that in a case like this, speaking in tongues is the Holy Spirit itself praying through human beings because they themselves are unable to pray, or express their sorrow and repentance as God wants them to do. And he referred to Romans 8:26 where Paul says, 'Likewise the Spirit helps us in our weakness; for we do not know how to pray as we ought, but the Spirit himself intercedes for us with sighs too deep for words.'

On the other hand, speaking in tongues can also express the highest degree of happiness, of praise to God for all he has done for his people. This, according to Timotheo Hezekiah Shitsimi, is the most common function of speaking in tongues when it occurs towards the end of a church service. People have come to the church to open themselves to receive the word of God. They have purified themselves, they have sung hymns and they have heard preaching. Towards the end they want to express their thanks to God for what he has given them in an even higher form than is possible through hymns, and this is made possible when they receive the Holy Spirit. Their speaking in tongues now becomes the most perfect form of praise, because it is the Holy Spirit himself teaching them how to bring their thanks to God.

Speaking in tongues does not only give people the ability to express their feelings towards God in the highest possible manner. It is also believed to be a means through which God can reveal things to humans beings (interview with Kefa Ayub Mavuru, 10 June 1975, and Thomas Malongo, 27 April 1975). This does not happen in all cases. Generally speaking, tongues serve to express people's emotions. In some cases, a person who is speaking in tongues is believed to reveal messages from God — this can be in the form of scripture from the Bible — or the person may receive the ability to disclose hidden sins, either his own or others', or a revelation about events which are happening or are going to happen in the future.

People can receive such revelations from God through speaking in tongues because it is believed that when they are possessed it is the Holy Spirit who speaks through them. It is the Holy Spirit who gives them the special language through which they can express their emotions, especially of great sorrow or happiness, to God. On the other hand, the Holy Spirit also brings revelations from God to human beings, in other words it is the mediator between God and his people. Only through the Holy Spirit is real communication between God and humans made possible, and this is why it is necessary for every Christian to receive it (interview with Timotheo Hezekiah Shitsimi, 3 June 1976).

Originally, speaking in tongues was always regarded in the way described above, as the Holy Spirit speaking through human beings. Therefore, if people believed they had received a revelation, for instance about someone else's sins, they would stand up openly in the congregation and relate what they had seen. Experience has shown, however, that such direct disclosures do not always serve to build the congregation, and nowadays most of what is believed to have been revealed through speaking in tongues is therefore not related to the congregation. The caution shown by certain leaders does not only apply to open disclosure of what has been seen. Some also now believe that speaking in tongues in itself may not in all cases reveal a message from God. Japhet Zale Ambula and Kefa Ayub Mavuru and, more hesitatingly, Eliakim Keverenge Atonya, caution that Satan may be at work when people speak in tongues, deceiving them into believing that what they experience is from the Holy Spirit (interviews with Kefa Ayub Mavuru, 10 June 1975, Japhet Zale Ambula, 2 May 1975, and Eliakim Keverenge Atonya, 27 June 1975). But only certain leaders appear to have come to this conclusion and the general attitude among the large majority of Holy Spirit people is still that speaking in tongues is the Holy Spirit speaking through human beings, giving them the power for true worship and for receiving revelations from God.

It has been seen above that the emphasis on possession as the true manifestation of the Holy Spirit was in opposition to the teachings of most missionaries of the Friends Africa Mission. Also, only in special cases did trances occur in the traditional Abaluyia culture, namely as a sign that someone had been chosen by the ancestors to become a diviner or rain-maker. But there was no group spirit cult in this area before the arrival of Christianity. And, as it has been pointed out, the reason why Arthur Chilson's message about the necessity of baptism with the Holy Spirit was so readily accepted by these people is to be found in their social conditions. The many changes introduced by the colonial administration broke down social relationships and created insecurity, and in this situation the experience of entering a trance and of speaking in tongues released the tensions that had been built up and gave to these people a new feeling of their own worth that enabled them to dispense with the security of the clan.

Dreams

Other phenomena, such as dreams and visions, have more of a parallel in the traditional culture of these people, though in the context of the Holy Spirit Churches they, too, are regarded as means through which the Spirit brings messages from God to His people. Traditionally, the Abaluyia people attached a good deal of importance to their dreams. Ordinary dreams were not regarded as significant, but sometimes the ancestral spirits of people were thought to come and talk to them while they were dreaming. Such dreams were often seen as a sign that the particular spirit was dissatisfied, and the person who had seen the dream would then go to a diviner to find out what to do to appease the ancestor (Wagner 1949: 210).

This parallels the way Holy Spirit people look at their dreams. Not all dreams are regarded as significant, at least not in theory. Manoah Lumwagi (interview, 23 June 1975) says that many are of no significance at all, but that some come from the Holy Spirit and others from the devil. The Gospel Holy Spirit of East Africa Church makes the distinction in a slightly different way. Here there are also three categories of dreams — those that come from God, those that come from the person in question and those about material things. But the last category is never regarded as important (information from leaders of the Gospel Holy Spirit of East Africa, 30 June 1975). As in the case of speaking in tongues, Kefa Ayub Mavuru (interview, 10 June 1975) and Japhet Zale Ambula (interview, 2 May 1975) also warn that some dreams may come through Satan pretending to be the Holy Spirit. It appears, therefore, that the Holy Spirit Churches make an attempt to distinguish between dreams from the Holy Spirit, which are seen as important for the Church, and those that are of no significance or even dangerous.

Sundkler makes a similar distinction in his description of the dreams he collected from Zionist Churches in South Africa. He points out that the dreams the Zionists regard as important follow a pattern, with certain elements being repeated from one dream to another (Sundkler 1970: 265). Although dreams in the Holy Spirit Churches appear to follow a less fixed pattern than they do among the Zionists, certain formal elements nevertheless also recur in a number of dreams by members of these Churches as well. As in South Africa, one such element is of a group of people standing near a stream. The colour white is also considered important to both the Zionist and the Holy Spirit Churches. The colour red features very rarely in Zionist dreams and when it does it symbolizes the fire of hell. In the Holy Spirit Churches, on the other hand, red and white are the only colours I have heard mentioned and, being the symbolic colours of these Churches, both are seen frequently. Mountains, the flag and the cross are other important elements in the thinking of the Churches that feature in dreams. My dream material was mostly collected from the Gospel Holy Spirit of East Africa because this is the only Holy Spirit Church in which dreams are still regularly recounted for the whole congregation to hear. It is interesting to note that Enis Kadali, the 'mother' of this Church, is quite often seen in the dreams of its members, probably because she symbolizes the Church as such.

The professed purpose of relating dreams openly in church is to see whether they reveal anything that can build the Church or that will encourage members to repent (Nathan Keya's invitation to members to recount their dreams and visions at a church service at the Endeli headquarters of the Gospel Holy Spirit of East Africa, 2 March 1975). And, in keeping with this, the contents of dreams often centre upon the subjects of defeating adversaries who threaten the Church, making the choice between belonging to the Church or to the world, and going to heaven, all themes that figure prominently in the thinking of these Churches.

On 15 June 1975 a woman member of one of the Holy Spirit Churches related the following dream during a meeting of the Gospel Holy Spirit of East Africa. She saw a very wide river. To the north it was white, to the south it was red and in the middle was a fire. She was standing on one bank with a large group of people, and somebody in the group asked, 'Where is the old woman?' When he had said that, a flag fell down in the river, and someone else now suggested they use the flag and flagstaff as a bridge to reach the opposite bank. On the other side of the river stood an old, tall man with a beard. He helped Enis across, and when she had reached the other side she stretched out her hand. Her arm was so long that it could reach across the river, and people now held her hand and were pulled by her to the opposite bank. When they came there, a young man who was sitting on a hill washed their hands, after which he asked them to sing and to carry branches of palm trees. They now picked flowers, which they found along a road, and marched forward, carrying the flowers and singing hymns. The interpretation of this dream by Zebedaioh Malolo, which followed shortly afterwards, was that the river symbolized the end of the world. The old mother, Enis Kadali, was the one through whom they had all become members of the Church, and she was also the one who would save them in the end.

It will be seen that the main theme of this dream is the question of how to reach the other side of the river, how to reach heaven. And Enis Kadali and her Church, symbolized by the red and white colours and by the flag and flagstaff, play a prominent role in leading the people across. Once they have reached the other side they are purified through the washing of hands, and they can now sing the happy hymns of heaven. The fire possibly symbolizes the fire of hell, and the hill on which the young man was sitting may be the holy mountain of God.

Another dream (told to me in a talk with leaders of the Gospel Holy Spirit of East Africa, 30 June 1975) was related by Petro Sida, who said that it had made him leave his sinful ways and decide to join the Gospel Holy Spirit of East Africa. As a young man, while his mother was still alive, he had been a member of the Holy Spirit movement, but when she died he left the Church and began to drink heavily. In this dream he was at a drinking party. At one side of the room sat the people with whom he was drinking, and at the other side sat women from the Church. They shouted to him, 'Petro, do you want to go and drink beer?' He answered, 'I want to drink tea.' But they shouted again, 'Your only work is to drink beer.' At this point his mother appeared in the room, dressed in a long, white garment with a cross. She said to him, 'I left you when you were a member of the Church. But now you have left it.' She then placed him among the people of the

Church and said, 'Forgive my son for what he has done.' From the moment he woke up from this dream he stopped drinking and became a member of the Church again.

This dream reflects the choice between two alternatives, an important feature also in Zionist dreams. The Church's moral prohibition against drinking figures prominently, and Petro's conversion is brought about through the mediation of his mother, who is dressed in the white garments of heaven, and of the Church.

Through such dreams the Spirit is believed to speak to the members of the Holy Spirit Churches and to guide them and their Churches along the right path. The dreams reflect the important symbols and beliefs of the Churches, and they therefore serve to strengthen the individual's sense of belonging to a particular Church and to strengthen group solidarity. When the Church's characteristics are seen to be sanctioned by the Holy Spirit itself through the dreams of its members, these dreams become important factors for the integration of the Church, just as dreams in the traditional culture, believed to bring messages from the ancestors of the dreamer, helped to preserve group solidarity within the clan community.

Prophecy
Prophecy is another important gift of the Holy Spirit, and the people who possess the ability to prophesy are given prominent positions in the Holy Spirit Churches. Prophecy cannot, however, be separated from the other gifts of the Spirit, for prophetic insights are revealed through these means, namely through speaking in tongues and through dreams and visions. Timotheo Hezekiah Shitsimi (interview, 3 June 1976) says that speaking in tongues and prophecy are basically the same, but with the difference that speaking in tongues is unintelligible except to a few people, while prophecy is spoken in a normal language and can be understood by everybody. In an interview on 10 June 1975, Kefa Ayub Mavuru, who is recognized as a prophet by the members of his Church (interview with Peter Ihaji, 25 June 1975), describes how he receives his prophetic insights in a very concentrated moment after he has spoken in tongues. Before being led to reveal what the Holy Spirit has shown him, he will feel very tense, with something approximating a pain in his stomach. Prophetic insights may also be revealed through dreams. This may be the case, for

example, when new hymns are given by the Holy Spirit to a member who is specially gifted in this respect (interview with Timotheo Hezekiah Shitsimi, 3 June 1976). Other kinds of prophecy may also come through dreams. In an interview on 2 May 1975, Japhet Zale Ambula said that any member can dream or see visions, but that some people see more than others through these phenomena, and such people are prophets (Jotham Eshera said the same thing in an interview on 8 March 1975).

Prophecy is described in different ways. Some say that a prophet is a person who is able to predict what will happen in the future (Enis Kadali in a talk with leaders of the Gospel Holy Spirit of East Africa, 30 June 1975). In an interview on 3 June 1976, Timotheo Hezekiah Shitsimi said that prophets can both see what is happening now and predict what will happen in the future. As an example, Enis Kadali mentioned that in the early days of the Holy Spirit movement one of them had prophesied that the Europeans would some day leave their country. There is also a very common belief that, through prophecies, the Holy Spirit indicates who the Churches' future leaders will be (information from Jotham Eshera, 8 March 1975, and Timotheo Hezekiah Shitsimi, 20 February 1975).

The most usual answer to such questions is that prophets are those able to interpret dreams and visions and to see other people's hidden sins. Generally speaking, they can see things that ordinary people cannot (information from Jotham Eshera, 8 March 1975), and this faculty enables them to interpret the dreams and visions revealed to Church members and to explain their significance for the individual or for the Church as a whole (interview with Kefa Ayub Mavuru, 10 June 1975). Japhet Zale Ambula (interview, 2 May 1975) says that the role of prophets is to see other people's sins, and others agree that this is a very important part of their work (talk with leaders of the Gospel Holy Spirit of East Africa, 30 June 1975). Because of their ability to see what is hidden from other members and to reveal what comes from God and what comes from Satan, the Holy Spirit Churches regard prophets as very important people. To Jotham Eshera (interview, 29 April 1975) 'they are the ones who can see which way the Church goes', and Timotheo Hezekiah Shitsimi believes that God will reveal to them what he wants the Church to do (interview, 3 June 1976). Without their guidance the Churches would be at a loss and without moral direction. According to Timotheo Hezekiah Shitsimi, for a properly organized Church the gift of prophecy is absolutely indispensable.

It appears that the functions of prophecy have gradually come to cover a more and more limited field. Prediction of future events is still mentioned, but the emphasis seems to lie on the prophets' ability to interpret dreams and visions and especially on their gift to disclose other people's hidden sins. This corresponds to a development common to all Pentecostal prophecy as described by Hollenweger. He writes that, generally, prophecy is seen as the ability to reveal future events and that its reliability can be recognized from the signs that it is fulfilled in due time. But older Pentecostal denominations reject prophecy as the foretelling of the future and permit it only as edification (Hollenweger 1972: 345).

An important reason for this development was that the whole movement had been badly shaken by a false prophecy during the early years of the Holy Spirit Churches. A man, who was recognized as a prophet, made public a revelation he claimed to have received from the Holy Spirit, which instructed all men who belonged to the Holy Spirit movement to send away their wives and take young girls instead (interviews with Eliakim Keverenge Atonya, 27 June 1975, Kefa Ayub Mavuru, 10 June 1975; information from Enis Kadali, 30 June 1975). A number of members followed his direction. However, it was not long before his prophecy was seen to be false and the men took back their former wives. This experience is often referred to as an example of a prophecy everybody accepted at first as having come from God, but which later proved to be an attempt by Satan to deceive them and to break up their movement.

Since then, whenever a prophet claims to have received a revelation about the future or about a new course to be taken by the Church, no immediate action is taken. The Church waits until the same prophecy has been repeated two or three times, preferably in the way that others see the same thing. Church elders will then look into it and try to judge whether what has been revealed will be beneficial to the Church and whether it is in accordance with the Bible. Only after such close scrutiny will the prophecy be accepted as a true one and be incorporated into the practices or beliefs of the Church (interviews with Japhet Zale Ambula, 2 May 1975, and Eliakim Keverenge Atonya, 27 June 1975). But nowadays this type of prophecy is rare; most are limited to the edifying revelations of the meanings of dreams and visions and of people's hidden sins.

Prophecy in the Holy Spirit Churches appears to fulfil approximately the same functions as two of the specialized 'offices' in the traditional Abaluyia culture, those of the diviner and of the dream-prophet. Biblical prophecy, in the sense of a critique of social conditions and how best to reform them, appears to be all but absent.

A dream-prophet, an *omung'oli*, is a person who is believed to possess the ability to foretell important events, both of a public and a private nature, by means of the inspiration received from the spirits of ancestors through dreams (Wagner 1949: 212). The prophet in the Church who predicts future events through inspiration received from the Holy Spirit fulfils the same function in the Church as the *omung'oli* did in the traditional clan community.

When prophetic gifts are described in terms of the ability to reveal what is hidden from ordinary human beings, a parallel can be seen in the office of the diviner in the traditional culture. Wagner (1949: 219) defines the work of a diviner, *omukumu*, among the Abaluyia in the following way:

> Divination ... aims at discovering mystical causal connections rather than at predicting future events which is predominantly the domain of dream-prophecy as well as of the inspection of entrails. While it is the first and foremost aim of divination among the Bantu Kavirondo to detect causes, its second, subordinate aim is the discovery of the appropriate measures which will serve to combat and neutralize the causes that have been detected.

Divination is used when misfortune of one kind or another has befallen a person or a family. The diviner will then try to discover which evil agent is responsible for the misfortune and, once the agent has been detected, will advise the clients on what countermeasures they have to take to drive out the evil so that normal conditions can be restored. In the same way, a prophet in one of the Holy Spirit Churches tries to detect the evil that influences individual members, namely their sins, and instructs them in the right way to repent and so to drive out the evil. The difference between the diviner and the prophet is that while the diviner is believed to be inspired by the spirits of ancestors when detecting the hidden causes of evil, the prophet is thought to be inspired by the Holy Spirit.

It has been seen, then, that dreams, prophecy and, to a limited extent, speaking in tongues have their parallels in the traditional religion of the Abaluyia people. The phenomena, which before were believed to be inspired by ancestral spirits, are now regarded as the gifts of the Holy Spirit which, through them, reveals what would otherwise be hidden from human beings and directs the Church and its members along the true way of God. This is not to suggest that the members of the Holy Spirit Churches themselves regard these phenomena as substitutes for those found in the traditional religions of their area. Church members are warned against consulting diviners, for example, as this would be equivalent to a denial of their Christian faith and a reversion to the worship of 'other gods' or of 'misambwa'.[1]

That parallels can be drawn with their traditional religion is an indication that, in seeking to know the will of God, the members of the Holy Spirit Churches experience His guidance through what are for them the most natural means of communication between the unseen world and human beings. By accepting the significance of these phenomena and incorporating them into their lives the Holy Spirit Churches help to integrate the thought patterns of their members into the whole of their Christian experience. They become Churches in which their members can feel at home and see the will of God revealed in ways that are meaningful to them.

At the same time, however, it must be remembered that these phenomena are not confined to African Churches. Speaking in tongues and prophecy are phenomena that can be found in Pentecostal type Churches anywhere in the world, and this shows that not only the traditional background, but also social conditions, are instrumental in the development of these phenomena. Hollenweger (1972) points out that Pentecostal Churches are often found among deprived people, where they serve to release the tensions of ordinary life and to give their members a new feeling of identity in a group in which they feel at home. The belief of the Holy Spirit

---

1. Expressions used by Timotheo Hezekiah Shitsimi and Kefa Ayub Mavuru, respectively.

Churches in the importance of the baptism with the Holy Spirit is therefore shaped by the interplay of two sets of factors. On the one hand, the traditional forms through which the Abaluyia people believed that God's will was revealed to them is reflected in these Churches and, on the other hand, the social conditions of the members create a situation in which these phenomena achieve importance as a means of satisfying their emotional needs.

The Holy Spirit as the Giver of God's Power
The gifts of the Spirit described above are not the only ones the Holy Spirit Churches recognize. All the gifts mentioned by Paul, for instance in 1. Corinthians 12, may be cited by these people (for example, by Timotheo Hezekiah Shitsimi in an interview on 3 June 1976) as gifts that are important in their Churches. But speaking in tongues, dreams and prophecy are the gifts that are mentioned by far the most often as proof that a person has been baptized with the Holy Spirit.

The reason such a strong emphasis is placed on these particular gifts is that, through them, a person is actually able to experience the presence of the Holy Spirit. When discussing his own Church's belief in the Holy Spirit, compared with that of other Churches, Musa Ndagona, a pastor in the Lyahuka Church of East Africa, said that members of other denominations claim to believe in the Holy Spirit, yet refuse to repent their sins and so therefore are never possessed by the Spirit. It is like a man who has ploughed his farm without planting anything, yet claiming that he has harvested. These people have not understood what is necessary for a true belief in the Spirit. They only believe that the Holy Spirit exists, he says, but they have never actually seen the Spirit coming to them (information from Musa Ndagona, 13 April 1975).

When the Spirit comes to members of the Holy Spirit Churches, what they experience is its strength and power — words used again and again in prayers and sermons. The Holy Spirit can be called 'Lord of power' (prayer at a Gospel Holy Spirit of East Africa service in Marukusi church, Lugari, 27 April 1975; people pray for strength (Holy Spirit Church of East Africa memorial service, Bukoyani headquarters, 15 March 1976); or are urged to equip themselves with the spear, the sword and the shield of the Spirit (sermon by Kefa Ayub Mavuru at an African Church of Holy Spirit service, Lugala headquarters, 1 January 1975).

The power and strength the Spirit gives them enables them to overcome all the evil that threatens them and to walk in the ways of God. People may pray, 'The one who divides people up, Holy Spirit, bang him!' (prayer at Gospel Holy Spirit of East Africa church service, Marukusi church, Lugari, 27 April 1975). Purification at the beginning of a meeting may take the form of a prayer to the Spirit: 'Holy Spirit, take care that all evils that come in may get out — *gi twulidzwe!*' (purification at Lyahuka Church of East Africa service in Chanda church, 9 March 1975). And the Spirit is the power that is able to drive out the demons which cause disease, so that the sick are healed (interview with Timotheo Hezekiah Shitsimi, 6 June 1976).

But the Spirit does not only defeat evil powers. It also gives its own power to its followers. It makes them leave their evil ways, such as jealousy, quarrelling, anger and worshipping *misambwa*, and fills them with love, peace, humility and perseverance (sermon by Kefa Ayub Mavuru at African Church of Holy Spirit service at Isikhi, Tiriki, 25 December 1974). It is what gives them the power to preach with righteous words (sermon by Timona Luvai Malao at Endeli headquarters of the Gospel Holy Spirit of East Africa, 6 April 1975), because it is the leader of the meeting (said at an African Church of Holy Spirit service in Dumbeni church, 28 March 1975). The Holy Spirit is therefore seen as the force that leads people to follow the way of God, as is sung in one of the Holy Spirit Churches' hymns: '*Roho wakhuhila khu injira imbya*', 'The Spirit has taken us to a new way.'

Its power may also be described in more mysterious ways, as when at a Lyahuka Church of East Africa sermon at Chanda church (13 April 1975), the pastor announced that he had been unable to read, but after receiving the Holy Spirit was suddenly given the ability to read the Bible. This reflects a tendency in the Holy Spirit Churches to value the mysterious gifts of the Spirit more highly than ordinary gifts. For example, Jotham Eshera (on 13 April 1975) said that when leaders are gathered for a committee meeting they only want to pray and to wait to hear what messages the Spirit will bring them. They do not want to think on their own, because what comes through reason is not recognized as coming from the Holy Spirit.

The belief in the power of the Holy Spirit to drive out evil and to lead its people, whether through ordinary or extraordinary gifts, parallels the emphasis on power in traditional religions in Africa. Tempels (1969) holds that power, or force, which is the word he normally uses, is *the* basic concept in Bantu philosophy. According to him, all beings, whether human, animal, vegetable or inanimate, possess a vital force. And these forces can influence each other. For man, this means that another human being or an ancestral spirit has the power to diminish or reinforce his or her vital force, either directly or through the intermediary of an inferior force, whether animal, vegetable or mineral.

This corresponds to Wagner's analysis of the interplay of good and evil powers among the Abaluyia people. He does not emphasize the words force or power. But he points out how a person can be harmed, directly or indirectly, by another human being or by an ancestral spirit, and when a case like that occurs, countermeasures must be taken. If the evil was caused by magic employed by another person, detection and destruction of the harmful magic or a reversal of its power to strike the originator are effective countermeasures. If the harm is believed to have been caused by an ancestral spirit, this spirit must be appeased by means of certain rituals, possibly a sacrifice (Wagner 1949: 95).

There was, therefore, in the traditional culture of the Abaluyia people, a constant interplay of forces, some trying to harm others and others trying to undo the harm, or to protect against it. This corresponds to the way in which people in the Holy Spirit Churches look at the role of the Spirit compared with the evil powers that threaten human beings. Here the evil forces are mostly depersonalized and described as Satan or demons, and no magic is employed. But the dynamics is the same, namely that evil forces must be driven out by good forces, in this case by the Holy Spirit. Protection against attacks by evil forces is found when the Holy Spirit possesses a person and thereby gives him or her its power to resist evil.

The Holy Spirit as the Spirit of God

There appears to be a tendency among members of the Holy Spirit Churches to regard the Spirit as a mystical entity by itself, capable of providing them with the power to overcome the evil forces that threaten them. Therefore, leaders make a point of emphasizing the connection between the Holy Spirit, God and Jesus.

The leaders often refer to John 14, especially v. 16–17, in which before Jesus died he told his disciples that he would go to heaven, but would send them a helper. This helper would be the Holy Spirit whom the world would not know, but they would know Him (Japhet Zale Ambula at memorial service at Bukoyani head-quarters of the Holy Spirit Church of East Africa, 15 March 1976).

Kefa Ayub Mavuru (in an African Church of Holy Spirit sermon at Isikhi, Tiriki on 25 December 1974) said that those people who do not know properly will say, 'We are the people of the Spirit.' But, he emphasized, the Holy Spirit is the Spirit of God. 'The Spirit is God. God the Father, God the Son, God the Spirit.' The official teaching of the Churches therefore stresses that there is an intimate relationship between the Holy Spirit and the two other persons in the Trinity.

This relationship is sometimes seen as so intimate that people make no clear distinction between the roles of God, Jesus and the Holy Spirit. On the one hand, they may, like Kefa Ayub Mavuru (in a sermon at an African Church of Holy Spirit service, Lugala headquarters, 1 January 1975) say, 'This will not be paid by the natural blood, but it will be paid by the Holy Spirit.'

On the other hand, the Spirit may be referred to as the 'saviour' (as in a Lyahuka Church of East Africa sermon at a service in Lukuvuli church, 2 February 1975). Or, alternatively, it may be described as an equivalent to Jesus in this respect, as when the Holy Spirit people sing in one of their hymns: '*Yesu wakhwasava khulanyola lihona*', 'Jesus to whom we have prayed will give us salvation', and immediately afterwards: '*Roho wakhwasava khulanyola lihona*', 'The Spirit to whom we have prayed will give us salvation.'

Leaders therefore emphasize the close relationship between God, Jesus and the Holy Spirit. The difference between them is often expressed in chronological terms. Timotheo Hezekiah Shitsimi describes the chronological relationship in the following way: 'The people who were together with God were called the people of God. The people who were together with Jesus were called the people of Jesus or Christians. And now, the people who are having the Spirit are called the people of the Holy Spirit' (sermon during African Church of Holy Spirit memorial service at Mukomari, Isukha, 1 February 1976). This distinction between the time of God, the time of Jesus and the present time of the Holy

Spirit is made very often by different leaders, and it illustrates both the parallelisms between the persons of the Trinity and the superior importance attached to the Holy Spirit.

For people living now the Spirit is the saviour. That is, it gives them the power to overcome all evil and to do what God wants them to do, what they must do to be accepted in heaven. It is absolutely essential for people to accept the Holy Spirit, because it is what they will 'use to go to heaven' (sermon by Japhet Zale Ambula at a church service at the Bukoyani headquarters of the Holy Spirit Church of East Africa, 18 January 1975). It is 'the ticket to heaven' (sermon during Lyahuka Church of East Africa service in Chanda church, 12 April 1975).

It is through the Holy Spirit that people nowadays see God and receive the strength to follow his commandments. Without it, people would have no hope of salvation. But with it, they have the assurance that God is near to them with all his power, which he uses to overcome the evil forces that threaten human beings.

Japhet Zale Ambula's 'We have seen God' (sermon at a church service at Bukoyani headquarters of Holy Spirit Church of East Africa, 18 January 1975) reflects the joy and assurance of salvation, which has been brought to these people through the outpouring of the Holy Spirit. Ever since the early days of the movement they could not be induced to deny the validity of their experience of the Spirit, because through it they felt the reality of God's presence.

McVeigh's analysis of the traditional belief in God among African peoples adds increased importance to this experience of his nearness in the Holy Spirit Churches. McVeigh finds that the traditional concept of God saw Him as at the same time near to human beings and far removed from them, and as both good and bad. In his imminence God was regarded as a threat to human beings, and they therefore tried to push him far away from them, to a place where he was so far removed that the belief in his goodness could be upheld (McVeigh 1974: 126).

Wagner is not directly concerned with this discussion, but it appears, nevertheless, that his analysis of the Abaluyia people's religious beliefs confirms that McVeigh's findings can be applied to them. He writes that there is very little mention of a High God among the Abaluyia and that he is only invoked at important occasions (Wagner 1949: 167, 290). The non-living agents who are normally believed to influence the lives of human beings are the ancestral spirits, and they are regarded as both good and bad (Wagner 1949: 159). Since they, according to Were (1973: 5), are seen as intermediaries between God and living men, their characteristics can probably also be taken to reflect the characteristics of God, as the Abaluyia saw Him.

The Holy Spirit people's experience that God is near them and that in his nearness He is absolutely good is thus a revelation of great importance. They no longer fear that God may be against human beings, for He has proved that He is on their side and gives them His power to overcome evil. They no longer need intermediaries because God is near through His Holy Spirit. Those who remain faithful to their experience of God's nearness and goodness through the Spirit, and who obey his commandments, feel assured of salvation; they know that He will accept them in heaven.

Baptism with the Holy Spirit is therefore *the* basic phenomenon in the Holy Spirit Churches. Through it the members experience God's presence and receive his power to overcome all evil. This is felt as a great and true revelation, one for which there was a real need because of their traditional conception of God as being at the same time far and near, good and bad. When they receive the outpouring of the Holy Spirit they also receive assurance of salvation. They do this in ways that are meaningful to them, for they have a parallel in their traditional religion where speaking in tongues, dreams and prophecy were also regarded as the means of communication between man and God. At the same time, the social conditions under which the Holy Spirit people live, with extensive changes and growing insecurity, increase the importance of these phenomena in that the tensions of everyday life are released and, through the fellowship of the group they bring together, enable these people to build a new identity. The interplay of these factors, the needs created by their traditional background and social situation, made the Holy Spirit people highly receptive to the message of the baptism with the Holy Spirit, even though this meant conflict with the Friends Africa Mission.

Purification

Confession as a Necessary Condition for Receiving the Holy Spirit
Arthur Chilson taught in 1927 that confessing all one's sins openly

was a necessary condition for receiving the Holy Spirit and, consequently, for reaching salvation. The Holy Spirit Churches have held on to Arthur Chilson's teachings and, for them, confessing their sins is therefore absolutely necessary for those who want to receive the Spirit. While discussing other denominations' belief in the Holy Spirit, Musa Ndagona said (on 13 April 1975) that they never actually see the Spirit coming to them precisely because they do not believe in the necessity of open confession: 'If the Holy Spirit is to come into somebody, he must cry with tears rolling on his cheeks, so that the Holy Spirit can enter into his heart. The Holy Spirit does not just come so easily.' Timotheo Hezekiah Shitsimi (in a sermon at an African Church of Holy Spirit service in Dumbeni church, 21 February 1975) described the relationship between confessing one's sins and receiving the Holy Spirit in the following way: 'This birth of the Spirit is a reward which comes from heaven to reach those who have confessed their sins.'

Confession in the Holy Spirit Churches is described in terms of purification from evil. Petro Sida, in urging people to confess, used the analogy of somebody washing with Lux soap. These people do not have Lux soap with which to wash their bodies, he said, but they shall wash their hearts instead and bring them before Jesus (Gospel Holy Spirit of East Africa church service in Marukusi church, Lugari, 27 April 1975). In fact, the word normally used to describe the rituals for driving out evil at church services is 'khwitakasa' which means 'to clean' or 'to wash'.

When purifying themselves people ask Jesus to forgive them for all their sins. They pray, 'Yesu yasamehe', 'Jesus forgive me', or they can say, 'We ask in Jesus Christ that all bad things and demons — gi twulidzwe!' (Thomas Malongo at a Gospel Holy Spirit of East Africa service at Endeli headquarters, 6 April 1975). Jesus is recognized as the one who brings forgiveness to those who confess their sins, as the one who can drive out the evil.

Leaders sometimes try to emphasize the connection between the death of Jesus and the purification which may be received by human beings. Kefa Ayub Mavuru says in a sermon of the African Church of Holy Spirit (at Isikhi, Tiriki, 25 December 1974) that Jesus poured his blood in order to wash our hearts. Therefore, those who believe in Jesus no longer have to perform sacrifices as the Israelites did. All that is necessary now is for people to repent their sins and thereby cleanse their hearts.

There is a strong tendency to look at purification as mankind's own work, as an automatic consequence of having confessed one's sins. As Timotheo Hezekiah Shitsimi said (at an African Church of Holy Spirit service in Dumbeni church, 28 March 1975), 'He died, so that our souls can get salvation. ... What you can do is to find out the sins which have always disturbed you.' The belief appears to be that the death of Jesus was a necessary condition for man's salvation, but that this salvation will only be realized if people themselves also do something. And what they can do is confess their sins. This is confirmed by the statement, quoted before, that unless people purify themselves they can have no hope of God answering their prayers: 'If you know that you have sins, and you kneel down with your sins, Christ will never come near to you' (call to confession at a church service at Lugala headquarters of the African Church of Holy Spirit, 20 March 1975).

The emphasis on people's own ability, and duty, to work towards their salvation comes out clearly when they are called to repentance with the words, 'Save yourself!' (Timotheo Hezekiah Shitsimi, memorial service of the African Church of Holy Spirit, Mukomari, Isukha, 1 February 1976). The Holy Spirit people sing: 'Repent while you are still here. When Jesus will call, you will be saved from the grave.' And in the following verse 'repent' is replaced by 'save yourself': 'Save yourself while you are still here. When Jesus will call, you will be saved from the grave.' Repentance and confession of sins will, almost automatically, lead a person to salvation. It is therefore not surprising that the word 'gi twulidzwe', as has been seen above, can be used as a kind of 'spiritual magic', as a word which, when uttered, will automatically drive out the evil. It has been seen also how the prayer 'Yasamehe Yesu' has in many cases developed into the artificial word 'osiwigisu' which, like 'gi twulidzwe' is used by many as a magic word, without thought of its original meaning.

The biblical basis for the emphasis on repentance in the Holy Spirit Churches is found in Mark 1:14–15 which says: 'Now after John was arrested, Jesus came into Galilee, preaching the gospel of God, and saying, "The time is fulfilled, and the kingdom of God is at hand; repent, and believe in the gospel".' Repentance is in these Churches interpreted as open confession of sins, and the understanding of this scripture is: 'Confess and believe in the Bible.' And the preacher who said this (at an African Church of Holy Spirit service in Dumbeni church, 21 February 1975) continued, 'You will never see the Holy Spirit without seeing the holy scriptures,' and, 'After you have believed in the scriptures, they will lead you to the Holy Spirit'.[2] In the end, he said, the Holy Spirit will lead you to Jesus. The confession of sins is therefore seen as a vital link on the way to salvation, which consists of confession, belief in the Bible, receiving the Holy Spirit, and, finally, seeing Jesus in heaven.

When the Holy Spirit people talk about the confession of sins as a necessary condition for receiving the Holy Spirit they often fail to mention the necessity of first reading the Bible. This may be brought in by certain leaders in an attempt to counteract the tendency among the members to look at repentance as a magic means, the use of which will automatically bring them possession with the Holy Spirit.

Purification through the confession of sins is therefore looked upon in the Holy Spirit Churches as the necessary condition for receiving the Spirit. Though the role of Jesus as the one who purifies because of his death is recognized, there is a strong tendency to see confession, with the use of special, powerful words, as a magic means through which human beings can themselves bring about purification, after which they automatically receive the Holy Spirit. To counteract this tendency, some try to speak about the Bible as a guide to the belief in the Spirit. But the strongest trend appears to be to see confession as a means through which people can 'save themselves'.

Purification as the Driving Out of Demons
The evil driven out when people purify themselves is often seen as the sins they have already committed. Many specific sins may be mentioned, the most common being anger, jealousy, backbiting, stinginess and lying. In this case, purification consists of asking Jesus for forgiveness for the sins committed, or the evil is believed to be chased out, possibly even from the book in which all men's actions are written down, when people shout '*gi twulidzwe*' (interview with Eliakim Keverenge Atonya, 27 June 1975).

---

2. This same scripture is often quoted. Elfas Ojiango Sagida used it in a sermon at a church service at the Endeli headquarters of the Gospel Holy Spirit of East Africa, 6 April 1975.

Even then, the background in the death of Jesus does not have to be forgotten. Japhet Zale Ambula says that '*gi twulidzwe*' cannot be said to everything, for instance not to bad weather conditions. But when it is said in connection with sin, people know it will be effective, because God has promised to forgive sins.

Not everybody agrees that '*gi twulidzwe*' cannot be used to drive away bad weather. Thomas Malongo (10 May 1975) claims that it is effective in removing all kinds of evil, even stopping hailstorms. Most leaders maintain, though, that purification and the saying of '*gi twulidzwe*' apply only to personal problems. This does not, however, mean that purification and prayer for forgiveness are identical. Kefa Ayub Mavuru (interview, 10 June 1975) cites various kinds of evil that can be chased out. If he happens to hear other people engaging in 'bad talk', he will say '*gi twulidzwe*' to ensure that the bad thoughts do not stay in him. He will also say '*gi twulidzwe*' if he has had bad dreams. After a collection in church, a prayer is said to ask God to bless the money. In most cases this prayer is preceded by a short purification ritual aimed at driving out the evil that might adhere to the money. The following prayer (heard at Gospel Holy Spirit of East Africa service in Ikuvu church, south Maragoli, 23 March 1975) is one such example:

Lord, demons in *sadaka* [collection], and suffering and disappointments, stinginess with negligence and backbiting, others and despising and pride — in Jesus Christ, the demons — *gi twulidzwe*! All these things, in Jesus — *gi twulidzwe*! In Jesus — *gi twulidzwe*!

Disease is also believed to be driven out of people when they are purified through prayer and shouts of '*gi twulidzwe*'. Timotheo Hezekiah Shitsimi (interview, 6 June 1976) claims that all diseases are caused by demons. They enter people when they have been weak in faith, when the angels and Holy Spirit have left them. The demons therefore have to be chased away again in order for the sick person to be cured.

These examples of cases requiring purification show that the evil that influences human beings and makes purification necessary is not confined to sins people have already committed. Potential sin, such as the evil which comes in when one hears the bad words of others, and which might eventually lead the hearer to sin, must also be chased out. The same goes for the evil that may hang on to the money collected in church because of the sins of the people who give that money, as well as for the evil that causes disease. Evil is therefore conceived of in very concrete terms, as an independent entity which can move into human beings and cause them to carry out evil actions, think evil thoughts or become sick. Evil can also move out of human beings and thereby threaten their surroundings. Evil consists of demons, '*mademoni*', which can possess human beings and be driven out again through purification rituals.

It can now be understood why purification is considered absolutely necessary for a person to receive the Holy Spirit. When evil is seen as demons that possess people, and when they are believed to enter them at those moments when the Holy Spirit has left them, the picture emerges of a continuous battle between the demons and the Holy Spirit for the power over human beings. There is not 'space' for both at the same time. People are either under the control of the Holy Spirit or under the control of demons. And once demons have entered them, the only way for the Spirit to regain control is through purification rites that drive the demons out, so that the person becomes open again to receiving the Holy Spirit.

As has already been seen, this conception of a battle between good and evil powers is found in the traditional Abaluyia culture, where evil persons and ancestral spirits were believed to have the power to harm another person, and where it was considered necessary to take countermeasures to neutralize the evil influence. In the Holy Spirit Churches the role of evil-minded persons or antagonistic ancestral spirits has been taken over by demons, while the normal condition, without the disturbance of any evil powers, is here secured through the control exercised by angels and the Holy Spirit.

Leaders of the Holy Spirit Churches recognize the parallel between their own purification rituals and traditional methods of removing evil. Both Kefa Ayub Mavuru (interview, 10 June 1975) and Eliakim Keverenge Atonya (interview, 27 June 1975) describe how sacrifices used to be performed to cleanse a particular person or family. The only difference, they say, is that nowadays no sacrifice is required to chase evil away, only words. But the purpose of the rites is the same.

Comparing the belief held in the Holy Spirit Churches about the necessity of purification before possession by the Spirit with that of the Friends Church, it will be seen that the notion is basically the same. The doctrine of the Friends Church is that the Holy Spirit is present in every person as an 'Inner Light'. But sins make people 'dirty', so that the light of the Spirit cannot shine through them. Only if they are 'washed' through repentance will the light shine again (interview with Charles Wakhisi, 24 June 1975). As has been seen, the disagreement between the Friends Africa Mission and the Holy Spirit movement centred on how to repent. But the fundamental belief in the necessity of repentance as such is shared by the two parties.

Whereas the Friends missionaries laid great emphasis on sin and personal guilt — repentance was seen only in terms of praying for forgiveness — the Holy Spirit people have widened the range of evil forces that must be driven out to enable a person to receive the Spirit. Already committed sins are very important even in these Churches and must be confessed. But to these are added potential sins, namely the demons that can both enter a person and cause disease.

This difference reflects a difference in the whole outlook on life between the missionaries and the members of the Holy Spirit Churches. Welbourn (1963: 21) compares the two outlooks in the following words:

> The difference between the old world and the new is that the one *exteriorizes* its own inner experience of mental life and makes the whole universe alive with arbitrary, personal wills: while the other *interiorizes* the mechanism, which it thinks it finds in the external universe, and attributes man's highest achievements of thought and feeling to gastric secretions.

For the missionaries who belonged to the 'new' world, the evil at work in the world was interiorized and therefore seen as man's personal guilt and sin. The members of the Holy Spirit Churches, for whom life is experienced as an interplay of external good and evil forces, cannot limit their understanding of evil to include only personal guilt. Their traditional outlook on life has been incorporated into their Church and has received a Christian interpretation, and they therefore attribute the evil they experience to external forces, to demons, while the good they see is attributed to angels or to the Holy Spirit. Their belief in demons as real, threatening, evil forces makes it natural for the Holy Spirit people to include in their range of evil, from which they must be purified, also those demons that have not yet caused them to sin, as well as those that threaten their health and well-being.

Purification from evil as found in the Holy Spirit Churches therefore has its background both in the teachings of the Friends missionaries and in the traditional culture of the members. Arthur Chilson's teachings gave the Friends' emphasis on repentance before receiving the Holy Spirit a different turn, in that he stressed that repentance must be expressed through openly confessing one's sins. His teachings were accepted by the Holy Spirit people. These open confessions, coupled with the traditional Abaluyia concept of evil as consisting of external forces that have to be driven out, often through man's own efforts, have somewhat distorted the Friends' understanding of the aims and means of purification. The aim is no longer exclusively seen as receiving forgiveness for one's sins. It has been widened to include the driving out of all the evil forces, now interpreted as demons, that can enter a human being. Although the expulsion of demons is believed to have been made possible through the death of Jesus, many members of the Holy Spirit Churches tend to look at open confessions as their own work, as a means through which they have been enabled to purify themselves and so to work their own salvation.

Forgiveness through the Death of Jesus

Though the Holy Spirit Churches place a considerable amount of emphasis on the Spirit, which they regard as the being in which God's presence resides in living people, these Churches still regard Jesus as a central figure in God's scheme of salvation. Jesus was the one who came to save people and, had it not been for him, the Holy Spirit would not have come.

What is emphasized about Jesus in these Churches is his death; his life is rarely discussed. Women sometimes preach about his birth and point out that he was born in the same way as any other child (sermon during church service at Lugala headquarters of the African Church of Holy Spirit, 26 December 1974), but this appears to be more of an appeal to the feelings of female listeners than an expression of any real understanding of the incarnation. References are sometimes made to Jesus's activities on earth. For example, in a prayer (during a memorial meeting at the Bukoyani headquarters of the Holy Spirit Church of East Africa, 15 March 1976), Isaiah Maleya referred to Jesus healing the sick and asked him to heal people today as he had done when he was on earth. But these sporadic allusions to the life of Jesus are very few, and it appears that the meaning of the incarnation, that in Jesus God became man, is of no significance to the thinking of the Holy Spirit Churches.

The important aspect of Jesus's coming to earth is his death. The story of his passion may be related in great detail, as in Timotheo Hezekiah Shitsimi's Good Friday sermon (at Dumbeni church, 28 March 1975) referred to above, and there are innumerable shorter references to how he died in order to save sinners. Jesus's death is believed to have benefited human beings in two ways: it enabled people to receive forgiveness for their sins and thereby become pure, and it opened the way for God to send his Holy Spirit to people who had been purified.

In his sermon at an African Church of Holy Spirit memorial meeting (at Mukomari, Isukha, 1 February 1976), Timotheo Hezekiah Shitsimi outlined the important points in Jesus's work of salvation. He was God. But from heaven he saw Satan disturbing people on earth, and therefore he decided to come to die on the cross. He was born by Mary like any other child, and when he grew up he preached for three years. But the Jews crucified him, and he died. On the third day he was raised from the grave and, after having been together with his disciples for 40 days, he went to heaven from where he will come back again. But before he went to heaven he told his disciples that he would not leave them as orphans, but would send them the Holy Spirit. And this Holy Spirit is what has now descended upon the members of the Holy Spirit Churches.

The reason why Jesus came to earth, and why he died, is here seen to be his wish to defeat Satan. And Satan is defeated by the Holy Spirit, as seen above. The birth of Jesus, his life, death, resurrection and ascension are all seen as necessary stages on the way to the most significant event: the outpouring of the Spirit on people on earth. The death of Jesus is therefore the fundamental act of salvation, since without it the Holy Spirit would not have come. Through his death Jesus has founded the true Church, the Church of the Holy Spirit.

It has been shown above that no human beings can receive the Spirit unless they have first confessed all their sins and been purified of the evil forces that threaten to overpower them. It was pointed out how members of the Holy Spirit Churches often regard confession as a means through which people themselves can bring about their own purification and so open the way for the Spirit to descend upon them. It has not, however, been forgotten that it is Jesus who forgives those who repent and confess their sins, as shown in the prayer '*Yesu yasamehe*', 'Jesus forgive'. Leaders often talk about how Jesus shed his blood to cleanse the hearts of people and to wash away their sins (as in Japhet Zale Ambula's sermon at a Holy Spirit Church of East Africa service at Bukoyani headquarters, 6 July 1975). The tendency to look at confession as man's means of 'saving himself' is, however, strong. The death of Jesus is still looked upon as the fundamental event to have made forgiveness and the defeat of Satan possible. Rather than believing that, because of his death, Jesus still forgives sinners even today, many members of the Holy Spirit Churches appear to look upon his death as the point at which a system was set up to enable people to purify themselves and so receive the Spirit and, ultimately, reach the final salvation in heaven.

In the Holy Spirit Churches, this aspect of Jesus's death, namely that it made purification possible, is seen to have performed the same function as both Old Testament and traditional Abaluyia sacrifices. For, like those sacrifices, it served to overcome evil. But Jesus's sacrifice of himself made all those other sacrifices unnecessary. The people who live now cannot be saved by the blood of bulls or rams, but only by the blood of Jesus (sermon by Japhet Zale Ambula at a church service at the Bukoyani headquarters of the Holy Spirit Church of East Africa, 18 January 1975). He performed the one sacrifice that was necessary, and thereby made it possible for the evil that threatens man to be driven away. Because Jesus shed his blood to wash our hearts, people need no longer perform sacrifices. All that is required of them now is to repent and confess their sins, to cleanse their own hearts (sermon by Kefa Ayub Mavuru at African Church of Holy Spirit service at Isikhi, Tiriki, 25 December 1974). The death of Jesus secured human confession as an effective means of purification.

This emphasis on the sacrificial aspect of Jesus's death is perhaps one reason why his resurrection is not seen as very important in the thinking of the Holy Spirit Churches. Though it is mentioned as one of the necessary stages between his death and his ascension to heaven, from where he sent the Holy Spirit, there is no mention of the resurrection as *the* event through which sin and death were overcome. His death on the cross alone made the defeat of evil forces possible, and, for the individual, the actual overpowering of evil is accomplished by following the way of repentance and receiving the Holy Spirit.

The death of Jesus is seen as having taken over the function of traditional sacrifices, which may be one reason why it is emphasized so much in the Holy Spirit Churches, at the expense of other aspects of his acts of salvation. Another important reason is that the Friends missionaries also regarded it as *the* fundamental event through which man received redemption from sin. The Holy Spirit Churches naturally took over many of the teachings of the mission from which they separated. And one of these, which has been incorporated as an important part of their system of beliefs, is the emphasis on the death of Jesus.

The hymns in the Friends hymn book, which are also sung by the Holy Spirit Churches, contain frequent references to the death of Jesus. An analysis of the nine most popular Friends hymns (Anon. 1958: numbers 1, 2, 5, 33, 40, 56, 57, 132 and 174) sung by these Churches[3] shows that his death is mentioned directly in four of them and indirectly in three of the others, in that they say that he overcame the sins of man. Another prominent theme in these hymns is the necessity of man's decision to follow Jesus who is now in heaven, but who will come again and save those who have been faithful to him.

It is perhaps significant that the Holy Spirit Churches' original hymns hardly mention the death of Jesus. Heaven, where those who have been righteous on earth will be accepted, is by far their most important theme. Though the focus on Jesus's death in the Friends hymns, which are sung as much as their own, may well have made the Holy Spirit people feel that it was unnecessary to repeat the theme in their own hymns, it may also have meant that His death is seen as the act through which man's salvation was

---

3. Those I have heard at least four or more times.

originally made possible, but that, for the salvation of the individual to be effectuated, it has to be supplemented with man's own acts of purification and with the power of the Holy Spirit. The Holy Spirit hymns then confirm that, though Jesus's death is the most important event surrounding His person and is essential for man's salvation, it is regarded as the starting point that set in motion God's scheme of salvation, which contains other elements too, rather than as the one, unique act of salvation.

The death of Jesus is therefore seen by the Holy Spirit Churches as the event through which God founded the true Church. It was a necessary condition for the coming of the Holy Spirit as well as for the purification of man, and without it the individual would have been unable to receive the Spirit. But there is little or no understanding of the significance of the incarnation. Jesus appears to be simply identified with God.

Because the Holy Spirit people fail to see the full significance of the death and resurrection of Jesus as the death and resurrection of God and man in one, there is little assurance that through these events the evil powers have really been overcome on behalf of every human being. Jesus's death is seen as the act through which God decided to defeat evil. Man is not believed to have been existentially involved and so the resurrection has lost its significance. This means that what was accomplished through the death of Jesus is seen to benefit human beings only because God wants it to do so, and this is probably why people's own ability to purify themselves has come to be looked upon by members of the Holy Spirit Churches as an important factor on their way to salvation. When they are purified and receive the Holy Spirit, they are assured that the evil powers that threaten them have been overcome. The death of Jesus is only the event which, in the first place, made purification and receiving the Spirit possible. It is not in itself the event which assures man of salvation.

Heaven as a Reward for the Faithful

Judgement According to Man's Deeds
The final stage of salvation, as seen by the Holy Spirit Churches, that which the other stages point forward to, is heaven. There are only two possibilities for man after his death: either he will go to heaven, or he will be sent to 'the sea of fire', to hell. The factor

that decides which of the two places he will go to is his behaviour while he is living on earth.[4]

It has been pointed out above how receiving the Holy Spirit is regarded as a necessary condition for going to heaven. It is 'the ticket to heaven'. It was shown that when people receive the Spirit, they see this as an experience of God's presence with them, and therefore they probably regard this possession as a foretaste of the life in heaven when they will always be together with God. This way of thinking is reflected in these people's use of the expression 'the seal' about the Holy Spirit. Timotheo Hezekiah Shitsimi (in a sermon at an African Church of Holy Spirit memorial service at Mukomari, Isukha, 1 February 1976) refers to Revelations 7:1–8 and says that the angels have been sent now to seal those who will be saved. And the seal by which these chosen ones will be known is the Holy Spirit.

The question arises, who are the chosen ones who receive the seal? Timotheo Hezekiah Shitsimi says that those on whom the seal will be found are the ones who follow the commandments of God, those who believe, those who are humble. It has been seen before that when people receive the Holy Spirit they are believed to receive its power. This is the power to resist all evil forces and to follow the ways of God. Members of the Holy Spirit Churches are therefore urged to walk together with the Spirit on the narrow path to heaven, the way characterized by repentance, purification, prayer and love, and by leaving behind quarrelling, theft, dishonesty and pride (sermon at a church service at the Lugala headquarters of the African Church of Holy Spirit, 20 March 1975). Unless people are faithful to their experience of the Holy Spirit, unless they come out of evil and walk in righteousness, 'hold the shield of the Spirit', they will not be accepted in heaven (prayer by Japhet Zale Ambula at a Holy Spirit Church of East Africa memorial service at Bukoyani headquarters, 15 March 1976).

There will be no mistake when a person's actions are judged. All he or she has done has been written down in a book in heaven. With reference to Revelations 20:12–13 Timotheo Hezekiah Shitsimi warns that in heaven there are two books. One is the

4. Timona Luvai Malao, for example, spoke of 'the sea of fire' in a sermon at a church service at the Endeli headquarters of the Gospel Holy Spirit of East Africa, 6 April 1975.

book of life, in which the names of those who have followed the commandments of God are written. In the other all people's bad deeds are written, and they will therefore not be able to escape the consequences of their actions (sermon at African Church of Holy Spirit memorial service at Mukomari, Isukha, 1 February 1976). Though people often talk about these books in heaven, the same idea is expressed in other ways as well. For example, a leader might say, 'What you do while on this earth will never go away', or 'pictures are taken of your words' (sermon at a church service in Lukuvuli church of the Lyahuka Church of East Africa, 3 January 1975).

People's actions are remembered and, when they die, everything they have done is looked into. The judgement as such is not described much by members of the Holy Spirit Churches. Timotheo Hezekiah Shitsimi (in a sermon at an African Church of Holy Spirit memorial service at Mukomari, Isukha, 1 February 1976) spoke of it as follows: 'God can see me all days. And he knows all the things that I do. . . . So there is nobody who can hide and say, I am not of God. All these people will go and stand before Jesus Christ who will be the judge.' In this quotation both God and Jesus appear to be looked upon as judges. What is seen as important is the belief in the judgement as such, not the way in which it will be carried out.

It may be significant that Jesus can be described as the judge because there is no talk of mercy in connection with the judgement. Once you have died, no more can be done to save you: 'Once you have entered the grave, there is no way to be saved again' (Timotheo Hezekiah Shitsimi in the same service, 1 February 1976). Your actions while you are alive are the only factor that decides whether you are accepted in heaven or sent to the sea of fire.

Heaven as a Happy Place without Suffering
The Holy Spirit people often describe how they imagine heaven to be. Heaven is contrasted with this world, which is seen as a place of suffering and difficulties (Timotheo Hezekiah Shitsimi, in a sermon at an African Church of Holy Spirit memorial service at Mukomari, Isukha, 1 February 1976), and as a 'desert' (Isaiah Maleya in a prayer at a Holy Spirit Church of East Africa memorial service at Bukoyani headquarters, 15 March 1976). In

this life the members of the Holy Spirit Churches are poor. They are the ones whom nobody respects. But these poor people are exactly the ones who will be saved (sermon by Timona Luvai Malao at a church service at Endeli headquarters of the Gospel Holy Spirit of East Africa, 2 March 1975). Scriptures are quoted to prove that this is not an empty hope, but that God himself has decided to save the poor. The most important scripture used in this connection is 1. Corinthians 1:26–9 (quoted at an African Church of Holy Spirit service at Dumbeni, South Kabras, 21 February 1975), since it reflects the Holy Spirit people's notion of themselves compared with the world around them:

> For consider your call, brethren; not many of you were wise according to worldly standards, not many were powerful, not many were of noble birth; but God chose what is foolish in the world to shame the wise, God chose what is weak in the world to shame the strong, God chose what is low and despised in the world, even things that are not, to bring to nothing things that are, so that no human being might boast in the presence of God.

Further proof of the validity of the belief that the poor are the ones who will be saved is found in Luke 6:20–3 (quoted at a Gospel Holy Spirit of East Africa church service at Endeli headquarters, 6 April 1975):

> And he lifted up his eyes on his disciples, and said: 'Blessed are you poor, for yours is the kingdom of God. Blessed are you that hunger now, for you shall be satisfied. Blessed are you that weep now, for you shall laugh. Blessed are you when men hate you, and when they exclude you and revile you, and cast out your name as evil, on account of the Son of man! Rejoice in that day, and leap for joy, for behold, your reward is great in heaven; for so their fathers did to the prophets.'

Heaven, where the poor expect to receive their reward, is pictured as a place where all the sufferings of this world will have been brought to an end. Heaven is the new Jerusalem, described in Isaiah 60 (quoted at Lyahuka Church of East Africa outdoor meeting at Chevakali, north Maragoli, 4 January 1975), where, as sung in one of the original Holy Spirit hymns, the springs have good water, the fruits are good, and the love of God is everlasting:

> Shidaho sho mwigulu
> Shili na matsi malahi.
> Nulitsyayo khunywa
> Shulinyola buluhu.
> Muloji hamba — hamba
> wiganire
> Hamba winjire Jerusalem imbya.'

English translation:

> The spring of heaven
> Has good water.
> When you go there to drink
> You will never feel thirsty.
> Witch come — come
> repent
> Come to enter the new Jerusalem.

The first two lines are changed in the following verses to:

> Matunda go mwigulu
> Gali na matsi malahi —
>
> The fruits of heaven
> Have good water

and

> Buyanzi bwa Nyasaye
> Nu bwe mihiga gyosi —
>
> The love of God
> Is everlasting.

In heaven there is no suffering and no death, only peace. It is a village made of gold, where all the dead will be together again in happiness (memorial meeting at Bukoyani headquarters of Holy

Spirit Church of East Africa, 15 March 1976). There the saved ones will see God face to face (prayer at Gospel Holy Spirit of East Africa church service, Ikuvu church, south Maragoli, 23 March 1975), and be together with him for ever (church service, Lugala headquarters of the African Church of Holy Spirit, 20 March 1975).

The notion of a life after death is not something new that was introduced into the way of thinking of the Abaluyia people by Christian missionaries. In their traditional religion, the continuation of life beyond death was taken for granted. When people died their spirits were thought to leave their bodies and go to live in the spirit land. As has already been seen, these spirits were believed to retain a certain relationship with the living. They could visit living relatives in their dreams, and had the power to influence their health and general well-being in a positive or negative direction (Wagner 1949: 159). But, as Mbiti (1969: 165) pointed out, this way of looking at life after death in the traditional African religions gave nothing for which to hope. There was no hope of resurrection or of a growing towards God. Rather, the existence of the spirits was thought to be timeless; they were believed gradually to lose more and more of their human nature, until eventually their individual characters were completely forgotten and they became incorporated into the collective body of impersonal spirits.

What was new in the missionaries' teaching, therefore, was their emphasis on heaven as a better place than the present world. They did not preach simply the immortality of the soul, but rather its resurrection to the highest salvation in heaven. A new hope was introduced, and this reinterpretation of their expectation of a life after death had a great impact on the people who came to form the Holy Spirit Churches.

As long as the traditional cultural pattern was untouched, as long as the life of the clan was still looked upon as an integrated whole, the old way of looking at life after death, as a continuation of the existence of the spirit in a spirit world that was not thought to be radically different from this world, was sufficient. But when the traditional patterns of life were broken down by the introduction of colonialism with its many and radical changes, this conception of life after death came to be felt as unsatisfactory. Many of the old institutions in which the spirits of the ancestors played an important role were broken down, and it was therefore difficult to uphold the belief in the spirit world in its old form.

At the same time, the missionaries came with their teaching about a future dimension of time in which this old world would come to an end and a new, perfect world would come into existence. In the colonial situation, with all the insecurity it brought to the Africans, this message was received eagerly because it created a hope that some day the oppression, moral evils and instability they were experiencing in this world would stop and a new, harmonious life would begin.

For the members of the Holy Spirit Churches, life is still filled with insecurity and moral dangers because of the many changes that take place in the modern world. The message about a new and better world is therefore as relevant to them now as it was at the beginning of colonialism. Their conception of the life to come is naturally shaped by their feeling of deprivation in this world. Heaven is seen as a place where there will be no more poverty and disease. There the soul will have plenty of all the good things, and the security of always being together with God. Hollenweger (1972: 418) points out that it is a general tendency in Pentecostal-type Churches to regard this world as 'an unsatisfactory first attempt on the part of God, as a first version full of mistakes, shortly to be followed by a second corrected edition'. This parallel between Holy Spirit Churches in particular and Pentecostal Churches in general confirms the theory that a strong emphasis on heaven as a contrast to this world of suffering is found in Churches whose members belong to the poorer layers of society, who need the comfort this belief in heaven can give them.

It was mentioned above that the future dimension of time was brought into the Abaluyia way of thinking by Christian missionaries. This was a revolutionary change in their thought patterns, and one they readily accepted because of the need for it created by their social situation. Mbiti (1969) has an interesting point of view on the introduction of a futuristic hope into a thought pattern that showed no concern for what lay beyond a few years. He holds that the traditional concept of time still plays an important role in people's way of thinking, and therefore:

> They need to see it [paradise] realized 'immediately' for it to have a real meaning. They cannot conceive of the possibility

that the end of the world is an ultra-historical myth which
cannot be fitted into the immediate conceptualization of
individual men and women. They wait for this goal to come,
but then they see their Christian relatives beginning to die.
There is disappointment from the second generation of
Christians onwards; and it is precisely at this moment that
separatism begins to take place.

(Mbiti 1969: 235)

Disappointment at the millennium not arriving immediately
may explain the creation of independent Churches in the first
place. It also explains what happens within already existing independent Churches. It was shown above how the African Church of
Holy Spirit celebrates the 'ascension' of each individual Christian
who dies on the fortieth day after burial. The background to this
practice is said by church leaders to be Christ's ascension to
heaven. Because Christ went to heaven on the fortieth day after his
burial, so too do Christians. It was also pointed out that this practice parallels a traditional ceremony performed to establish a dead
person's status in the spirit world. But Mbiti's analysis of the
importance of the time dimension for the eschatological hopes of
African Christians gives an additional explanation for this
practice.

Originally, members of the Holy Spirit movement believed the
end of the world was imminent and that the millennium would
arrive within a very short time. When this failed to happen, they
had to adjust to life in this world and the millennial hope was
reinterpreted — the golden age came to be looked upon as a
completely different, other-worldly sphere, as heaven where the
souls of the dead would be happy for ever. But, as Mbiti points
out, people need paradise to be realized immediately. Though
members of the Holy Spirit Churches have come to accept the
future dimension of time, they find it difficult to conceive of the
end of the world as being so far away that it lies beyond the
history of this world. By believing that an ascension to heaven
occurs 40 days after death, the need for an immediate realization
of the millennial hope is fulfilled. And this belief is not felt to be
an artificial new doctrine. On the contrary, it fits into people's
traditional ideas about the stages through which dead spirits travel
to reach their proper status in the spirit world, and it has a biblical

justification which makes it acceptable as a specifically Christian belief.

Though, as in Timotheo Hezekiah Shitsimi's sermon (African Church of Holy Spirit memorial meeting, Mukomari, Isukha, 1 February 1976), Holy Spirit people sometimes talk about the end of the world and about how Jesus will come to take His people to heaven, it is doubtful whether this is seen within the context of the history of the world as such. Heaven is most commonly described in static terms, as a place where God and Jesus live and where the souls of dead people are accepted if they have been righteous during their lives on earth. Timotheo Hezekiah Shitsimi (interview, 6 June 1976) confirms the correctness of this last interpretation by saying that, for each individual person, the world comes to an end when he or she dies. This individual concept of salvation makes possible the almost immediate realization of the millennial hope.

The belief in the final salvation of man's soul in heaven is therefore very important in the Holy Spirit Churches. Though the notion of a life after death is not new to the Abaluyia people, what is new is the introduction of a future dimension of time, which promises them something better than their experiences on earth. This new aspect was brought in by the missionaries. But the old concept of time, which only takes the immediate future into account, lingers on, and salvation is therefore not seen in terms of a total destruction of the world and creation of something completely new at the end of history. It is understood as the soul of the individual going to heaven, conceived of non-historically as a specific place.

The Great Enemy: Satan

I have already described how the fight against evil forces is at the centre of the beliefs and religious practices of the Holy Spirit Churches and how, for a church service to be conducted in the right manner, it is essential to hold purification rituals at a very early stage, so that any evil that might interfere with the meeting has been driven out of the church. Unless this purification takes place, no individual member can receive the Holy Spirit and the meeting as such has no hope of God's blessing.

This emphasis on purifying oneself of already present evil forces, and resisting those that have not yet entered, needs to be seen against the background of a belief in a multitude of evil powers continually threatening human beings. Evil powers may try to come into the church to break up the meeting, or Satan may be standing just outside the church, waiting for people to come out from the meeting (Kefa Ayub Mavuru at a church service at Lugala headquarters of the African Church of Holy Spirit, 26 December 1974). Alternatively, Satan may occupy their houses while they are at church, so that as soon as they get home domestic matters make them forget all they said and heard during the service (sermon during church service at Lugala headquarters of the African Church of Holy Spirit, 20 March 1975). Satan may also appear to people in their dreams, pretending to be a messenger from God, because, according to 2. Corinthians 11:14, he is able to disguise himself as an angel of light (interview with Kefa Ayub Mavuru, 10 June 1975). He makes people 'blind' so that they worship *misambwa*, believing they are doing the right thing (prayer by Japhet Zale Ambula during memorial service at Bukoyani headquarters of Holy Spirit Church of East Africa, 15 March 1976), and he confuses people, so that they tell lies, get angry, steal, backbite or become jealous (interview with Eliakim Keverenge Atonya, 27 June 1975).

There are various names for these evil forces that are always threatening people. The term Satan, which has already been mentioned a number of times, is heard very often. Other names are 'the enemy', 'the bad spirit', 'the confuser', 'the evil one' or 'the wrong-doer'. Plural forms are also used, the most common being 'demons' and 'enemies'. These names are used interchangeably; whether one or the other is used appears to makes no difference to the essential meaning of a sentence. All the singular forms are different names for Satan. According to Timotheo Hezekiah Shitsimi (interview, 6 June 1976), the relationship between Satan and the demons is that Satan is the evil one in the true sense of the word, the holder of all evil power, but he has his 'angels', and they are the demons.

Members of the Holy Spirit Churches do not have very much to say about the origin of this evil power. Some people's remarks seem to reflect the opinion that Satan had one time been with God in heaven, but that he had come down from there to exercise his evil influence among people on earth. One woman (in a sermon at a church service at the Lugala headquarters of the African Church of Holy Spirit, 20 March 1975) said that, 'Satan asked permission from God to come down in order to tempt *avahuji* [separatists].' This corresponds to the conception of the origin of evil Wagner reports among the Bukusu, one of the Abaluyia tribes. He writes that a black or evil god, '*wele gumali*' or '*wele evimbi*', is thought to be the most important opponent of the High God, '*Wele Omuwanga*', the White God. He was created by the High God and was at one time living together with him. But when the High God discovered his evil actions, he drove him away from his own abode, and he is now living in lonely places, from where he comes to do people harm (Wagner 1949: 175). Although Wagner mentions this belief among the Bukusu only, it was very likely shared by other Abaluyia tribes, so that this myth about the origin of evil is what is reflected in the remarks that can be heard in the Holy Spirit Churches.

Similarly, the black god, like the High God, was believed to have helpers, evil-minded spirits that sent misfortune, sickness and death to the living. This corresponds with the multitude of evil forces the Holy Spirit people believe in, with the demons seen as the 'angels' of Satan. Although Western missionaries talked more about Satan than about demons, the belief in them is certainly not unbiblical.

Satan, or the demons as his agents, can lead people to commit sins. As has already been seen, he can also cause disease, or even death. Similarly, he may bring disease and death to animals (interview with Timotheo Hezekiah Shitsimi, 6 June 1976), or he may cause somebody to lose a job (interview with Japhet Zale Ambula, 2 May 1975). Satan thus exercises his evil influence on both the spiritual and material aspects of people's lives. If a cow dies, it may, according to Timotheo Hezekiah Shitsimi, be interpreted as Satan tempting the owner of the cow. Satan is then seen as having brought disease and death to the animal in an attempt to weaken the owner's faith in God's protective power. On the other hand, Japhet Zale Ambula says that a man who has lost his job and is unable to get another must first review his relationships with other people and confess his sins, before the people of the Church can pray for him. Satan's ability to harm people on both the spiritual and material levels of their existence is therefore not seen as two different ways of bringing the evil influence to bear upon them. For the Holy Spirit people, the spiritual and material aspects of life are closely connected. Material evil can lead a person to sin, and sin can bring about material evil. A threat against man's welfare in this life may at the same time be a threat against his eternal salvation, and Satan is active against both.

The ever-present evil powers, Satan and his demons, threaten all aspects of human life and must therefore be driven out and made harmless. It has already been seen that all evil is thought to be chased away, from the individual or from the church, through the purification rituals at church services. People also purify themselves outside church, if they have had a bad dream, if they have heard 'bad' talk, if they have committed a sin, or if they have fallen ill. Whatever evil influences they have felt must be driven away, so that the Holy Spirit can come to them again with all its power. Only it can give them the power to resist evil forces and act righteously.

Traditionally, if some misfortune occurred, the Abaluyia people would go to a diviner, an *omukumu*, to discover the agent responsible for bringing the evil to this particular person or family, and to find out what countermeasures to take. After consulting the diviner they would then carry out the prescribed countermeasures, possibly with the help of another specialist (Wagner 1949: 219). But for members of the Holy Spirit Churches, this way of combating evil is out of the question if they want to remain faithful to their Church. Consulting a diviner, or using any other traditional means of overcoming evil, is equivalent to 'worshipping other gods'. This sin, together with murder, adultery and robbery, is considered a 'sin of death', for which the sinner must be excluded from the community of the Church for a certain period of time and, before being accepted back into its fellowship, must confess in front of everybody (interview with Timotheo Hezekiah Shitsimi, 6 June 1976).

Although the means of combating evil in the Holy Spirit Churches are different from traditional ones, the terminology used in purification rituals and prayers suggests that people's ideas about how Satan is overcome to a certain extent still follow traditional patterns. One way of describing his defeat is to say that he is pushed away by God (prayer during an African Church of Holy Spirit service at Isikhi, Tiriki, 25 December 1974). The same basic concept appears to be behind all the purification rituals, in that the bodily movements of people when they drive the evil out of the church imply that they actually push it out. This corresponds to the traditional notion that harmful magic could in some cases be rendered ineffective if it were simply removed (Wagner 1949: 257). But sometimes it was necessary to destroy the magic, and this idea is also reflected in the Holy Spirit Churches, as when people ask God to 'spoil' the enemy (prayer at a church service at Endeli headquarters of the Gospel Holy Spirit of East Africa, 6 April 1975). The same idea, but possibly also that of reversing the direction of the evil magic to harm its perpetrator, is expressed by Holy Spirit people when they ask God to bring disease, war and famine to their enemies (prayer during memorial meeting at Bukoyani headquarters of Holy Spirit Church of East Africa, 15 March 1976), or to break the enemy's legs (prayer during church service at the same church, 6 July 1975), or when they pray, 'Those who are making traps, so that we can fall in them, let them fall in them themselves' (prayer during church service at the same church, 18 January 1975).

These comparisons between purification rituals and prayers in the Holy Spirit Churches, and ways of overcoming evil in the traditional Abaluyia culture, should not, however, be taken too far. While the terminology used in the Churches suggests that the old structure of thinking about these matters still exists, the differences between the old and new systems are greater than their similarities. The Holy Spirit Churches do not allow their members to use any extra help in chasing out Satan or the demons. Jesus had performed the one sacrifice that was necessary to overcome Satan and, for those who believe in him, confession and prayer are the only possible means of combating evil. If people have truly confessed all their sins, the Holy Spirit will come to them, and will give them the power they need to defeat Satan. Despite a tendency in these Churches to see purification as man's own doing, the basic belief is that Jesus made confession and receiving the Holy Spirit possible, and the Holy Spirit is what gives people the power to resist Satan. It is God himself who fights on the side of man against Satan, and the final defeat of all evil has therefore been secured for those who remain faithful to God. For the Holy Spirit people, there is still a very real battle going on in the world between good and evil powers, as there was in their traditional religion, but through the Holy Spirit they have received assurance that the all-powerful God is near to them, and that he is completely good. Therefore, they can now believe that he fights Satan on their behalf, and through them, and that eventually, in heaven, Satan will be completely defeated.

To sum up, then, the Holy Spirit Churches believe that multiple evil forces continually threaten human beings. While these may be called by different names, the real evil, in the true sense of the word, is Satan, who is assisted by numerous demons. Because these evil forces can attack people both spiritually and materially, they are an ever-present threat to all aspects of life. They have to be fought against and defeated. In driving away evil influences, members of the Holy Spirit Churches are not allowed to use any traditional methods. They have to rely solely on the means instituted by God when he sent Jesus to die on the cross. All they can do is confess their sins, purify themselves of all demons and live a righteous life. But God made purification possible and gave man the power to follow the ways of the righteous, so, although other agents and forces are involved, the fight between good and evil in the world is, ultimately, a battle between God, fighting for man's salvation, and Satan, trying to undo God's work.

God: The Giver of All Things
When the missionaries of the Friends Africa Mission came to western Kenya, their aim was to preach the salvation of man's sinful soul through the death of Jesus Christ. Like other missionaries, in their practical work, they also took an interest in the material aspects of people's lives. Because their message was based on the evangelical revival in Europe and America, the central theme in their preaching was the salvation of individual people, so that their souls would go to heaven when they died.

As seen above, this message introduced a new dimension into the Abaluyia people's thinking. It showed them a future dimension of time and gave them the hope that a better life was in store for them if they followed the ways of God. The missionaries' message was readily accepted at this time because the colonial administration had brought new strains and insecurities to people's lives. The hope of heaven assured them that their sufferings would come to an end and a better life would follow.

This belief in heaven is very strong in the Holy Spirit Churches. But although the members of these Churches attach great importance to the salvation of man's soul after death, they do not see

God's work with them confined to the other-worldly sphere. Satan is thought to exercise his evil power over all aspects of life, threatening both people's eternal salvation and their well-being on earth. Correspondingly, God is regarded as powerful enough to fight and defeat Satan in all spheres.

God is concerned about the salvation of man's soul. It was God who decided to send Jesus to die on the cross and thereby to show the way to salvation. Because of the death of Jesus, people are able repent their sins and confess, knowing that God will cleanse them of the evil powers that threaten them. Through the death of Jesus the Holy Spirit came to earth and is now given to those who have truly confessed all their sins, whereby they receive the power to resist the attacks by Satan, to be righteous, and eventually to go to heaven.

God is also believed to be concerned about man's well-being. The Holy Spirit people pray to him to be healed when they are sick (church service at Endeli headquarters of the Gospel Holy Spirit of East Africa, 6 April 1975) and to conceive children when they are barren (Lyahuka Church of East Africa service, Lukuvuli church, 2 February 1975). They pray for children to get the knowledge and understanding to do well at school (interview with Timotheo Hezekiah Shitsimi, 6 June 1976) and for the jobless to find work (church service at Bukoyani headquarters of Holy Spirit Church of East Africa, 18 January 1975). They ask God to bless their crops and their animals (church service at Marukusi church (Lugari) of the Gospel Holy Spirit of East Africa, 27 April 1975) and to give them rain so that they can harvest their fields and avoid starvation (memorial service at Bukoyani headquarters of Holy Spirit Church of East Africa, 15 March 1976).

God's active care for the material aspects of people's lives was not important in the missionaries' teachings, but was emphasized in the traditional religion of the Abaluyia people, as well as in the religions of other African peoples. Mbiti says that God is regarded as the creator of all things, but not in the sense that He created once and then withdrew from participation in the affairs of the world. On the contrary, He sustains His creation. He provides rain; he gives fertility to humans, animals and fields; he protects their health; and he gives them food and everything else they need (Mbiti 1969: 39). Wagner confirms that God is looked upon in this way among the Bukusu, where he is seen as both the creator and the minder of his creation (Wagner 1949: 167). Though he claims to have been unable to discover much about Logoli traditional beliefs in a High God, his description of a tribal sacrifice among these people, which was performed twice a year to secure a successful harvest and was addressed to the Supreme Being, suggests that the belief in God's power to sustain His creation is held by all the Abaluyia people (Wagner 1949: 290).

In the Holy Spirit Churches, the two aspects of God's work with His people, His care for their spiritual as well as for their material welfare, have been integrated into one set of beliefs. Discussing Baëta's (1968) criticism of African independent Churches for being so occupied with Christianity as a power to overcome the ills of the secular aspects of life that they do not fully understand the importance of repentance of sin and a life in faith, McVeigh (1974: 172) points out that the two emphases need not necessarily be placed in opposition to one another. He continues, 'There seems no good reason to indicate that the God who is concerned about man's sin is not also interested in his poverty and unemployment, and not merely in a secularized Western sense which strips these of their spiritual implications.' While Western man tends to see life as divided into two spheres, spiritual and secular, McVeigh argues that God is concerned about both, for, contrary to what Western man normally believes, the secular sphere is not in fact devoid of spiritual implications.

The Western way of thinking is alien to the members of the Holy Spirit Churches. For them, life is an integrated whole, and the God who is seen as powerful enough to secure man's eternal salvation must therefore also be concerned with people's lives here on earth. It has been seen how this concept of life as a whole is reflected in their ideas about the interaction between the secular and spiritual aspects of evil, so that the death of a cow may be seen as Satan tempting the owner, and, on the other hand, a man's unemployment is believed to be connected with the sins he has committed. God is believed to be sufficiently powerful to overcome both kinds of evil. The Holy Spirit people do not conceive of God as acting in two different spheres. They make no distinction between secular and spiritual spheres, and therefore God's actions to sustain man's material well-being are at the same time seen to cleanse him from sin, and vice versa, as shown by the following part of a prayer by Isaiah Maleya at a memorial service at the

Bukoyani headquarters of the Holy Spirit Church of East Africa (15 March 1976):

> This morning we cry to you: open heaven. Open heaven. Open heaven. So that the rain may rain. So that the rain may rain. The orphans will be happy, and they will praise you. Father, Son, and Spirit, Lord, listen. Lord, listen. Lord, listen. Lord, listen. Even when we have done that which does not please you, forgive us. Those who are sick, have mercy upon them. Open heaven and let the rain pour.

Evil powers cause man to sin and to become sick, and they also cause heaven to close so that the rain does not come. There is a connection between these different evils. Man's sins may account for God deciding to hold up the rain, which is why it is necessary to pray for forgiveness at the same time as praying for rain.

For the Holy Spirit people life is an integrated whole, and God has the power to defeat Satan and his demons irrespective of what aspect of man's life is being threatened. This belief, though blended into their Christian faith, and with the added dimension of salvation in heaven, is not very different from that found in the traditional religion of the Abaluyia people. The main difference between the old and new belief in God is that he is now thought to be near enough for people to approach him directly, and as often as they wish. Traditionally, the Abaluyia could also pray directly to God, but it was normally only done on special occasions, such as the birth of a child, a circumcision, a marriage, a funeral, or at harvest time (Mbiti 1969: 59). There was a fear in traditional African religions that, in his immanence, God could pose a danger to human beings if he came too near (McVeigh 1974: 126),[5] which was why he was normally approached through intermediaries in the form of ancestral spirits (Were 1973: 5). The Holy Spirit people feel God's presence very intensely when they are possessed by the Spirit, but they have been assured that this is a wholly good, powerful God who defeats all evil on their behalf, so there is therefore no longer any need for intermediaries. People can, and do, pray directly to God. Nonetheless, there are traces

---

5. Mbiti (1969: 43) also mentions that God may be thought to bring afflictions to people.

left of the belief in intermediaries, as when Isaiah Maleya prays to Daniel and Jacob,[6] but I have only heard this kind of prayer a couple of times and, in general, it can be said that the Holy Spirit people do not believe in any intermediaries between God and human beings.

They accept that the God in whom they believe is a Trinitarian God, and, as has been seen, they ascribe different functions to the three persons of the Trinity. Jesus was sent by God to make it possible for people to seek purification from the evil powers that possess them, and he in turn sent the Holy Spirit, which now brings God's power to human beings. But, basically, the three are one, and the same prayer may be addressed to all of them, as exemplified in the prayer above in which God, the Son, and the Holy Spirit were asked to bring rain, to forgive sins and to heal the sick.

This Trinitarian God — who created the world, came to earth in the person of Jesus to die so that man could receive salvation from the power of Satan, and who sent the Holy Spirit to effectuate this salvation — is the God who is near to human beings, and who is always on their side in their continuous battle against Satan. They may approach him with all their problems, without any distinction between secular and spiritual aspects of life. God is concerned with all spheres of human existence. He forgives man's sins, and he brings him health, fertility and rain. The Holy Spirit Churches have thus integrated the missionaries' message about the God who forgives sin and saves man's soul into their members' traditional belief in a God who sustains his creation and gives people all they need in life. God is believed to be concerned with the whole of life, and the Holy Spirit people

6. Daniel Sande and Jacob Buluku, the two great personalities when the Holy Spirit movement started in south Maragoli. The prayer was heard at a memorial service at the Bukoyani headquarters of the Holy Spirit Church of East Africa, 15 March 1976.

have therefore overcome the false distinction between secular and spiritual which is so common in the Western world, and which was introduced into the Churches in Africa by Western missionaries.

Conclusion

The history of the Holy Spirit Churches, as related in this book, has shown that the reasons for their coming into existence conform to the general theory of the writers who have dealt with this problem: that independent Churches are created in response to a social situation of insecurity or deprivation. In the case of the Holy Spirit Churches, this situation was brought about by the many and radical changes that were introduced by the colonial administration.

The people who formed the Holy Spirit movement were all Christians, having been converted by missionaries of the Friends Africa Mission. But the introduction of a colonial administration had broken down the unity of secular and sacred that existed in the traditional culture of the Abaluyia, and although Christianity was believed to be the religion that could recreate this unity in the new society, the missionaries' alliance with the colonialists was felt to hinder the realization of this unity. The missionaries were seen as part of the colonial establishment, and their paternalistic attitude towards Africans prevented the converts from participating fully in the affairs of the Church.

Therefore, when Arthur Chilson preached about the baptism with the Holy Spirit, many African members of the Friends Church eagerly grasped the opportunity this afforded for independence from the missionaries and for their own real involvement in the Christian life.

At first, these people had no intention of forming an independent Church. But when they were unwilling to renounce their new experience, this led to their expulsion from the Friends Africa Mission. The Holy Spirit movement can be seen as an unconscious protest against that part of the colonial establishment with which these people had had the closest contact, namely the missionaries. But their movement was not felt by the Holy Spirit people themselves as a protest. Rather, they wanted it to be a revival of the whole Church. They experienced the outpouring of the Holy Spirit as God himself present among them, as a revelation they could not deny without denying God. But it was, nevertheless, a protest against the missionaries because the Holy Spirit people refused to bend to their demands that they give up their new practices.

When the Holy Spirit people were expelled from the Friends Africa Mission, they did not at first know what to do, since their intention was not to form a Church of their own. Because of this lack of direction they isolated themselves from the rest of society for a number of years, concentrating only on confessing, praying, praising God and receiving the Holy Spirit. This was seen by the government, also, as a form of protest, as a refusal to bend to any authority except that of the Holy Spirit, and they were therefore closely watched.

The theory put forward by Peel, Ranger, Welbourn, Worsley and Wipper, that independent Churches are protest movements, although passive ones, is confirmed by this analysis of the background to the rise of the Holy Spirit movement. Wipper and Worsley mention that a characteristic of such movements is their hope for the imminent end of the world and the coming of the millennium. This can be observed also in the Holy Spirit movement, which explained its own isolation in terms of its belief that the world was coming to an end and so the only important thing to do was to worship God. Worsley mentions the crisis that arises in such movements when, after a number of years, the world continues: the expected millennium has to be reinterpreted, removed to another sphere, and the movement has to adjust to the society around it.

This is exactly what happened in the Holy Spirit movement. As the millennial hope faded, the Holy Spirit people became more and more aware of the need to find a way of living with other people. And, correspondingly, it became important for them that their movement be recognized as a Church. Therefore, they gradually developed more fixed organizational forms, until a point was reached when they received government registration and were accepted as Churches, equal to the mission Churches.

The more the Holy Spirit Churches opened up to the outside world, the more the government's former watchful attitude towards them relaxed, and this made many people join them who, before, had feared to do so. The question then arises of why so many people found, and still find, the Holy Spirit Churches so much more attractive than the mission Churches. One reason is that their emotional church services provide an outlet for people from the strains of their everyday lives. The shared experience of possession by the Holy Spirit creates a fellowship among members, which is important in the modern world where traditional fellowships in the clan are increasingly breaking down and thereby denying individuals the chance of realizing an identity through their specific position in the extended family or clan. The Holy Spirit Churches provide a new identity for their members. As a recipient of the Holy Spirit, everybody has a value and practically everybody has some kind of leadership role in the Church, which helps enhance his or her feelings of self worth. In addition, special clothes and ways of behaving, such as clapping instead of shaking hands when greeting, strengthen the individual member's identification with the Church.

The reality of the fellowship in the Holy Spirit Churches is expressed in various ways. These Churches perform ceremonies for their members at crucial stages of their lives, thereby showing their concern for each member. And the individual congregations are so small and intimate that no member is lost sight of by the others. Their problems, whether disease, sin, their children's performance at school or any other, are known by the leaders and by the other members of the congregation. The leaders pray for their spiritual and material well-being, either in the church or in their own homes. The Holy Spirit Churches therefore care for all aspects of their members' lives, and this concern, even for their material well-being, is expressed also in the cooperation that takes place among members for practical purposes, such as collecting money for a funeral or helping the sick.

In caring for both the spiritual and material aspects of their members' lives, the Holy Spirit Churches have recreated the unity of sacred and secular, which was characteristic of the traditional culture of the Abaluyia people. At the same time, they have made possible a true fellowship between members, similar to that of the former clan. The Holy Spirit Churches therefore fit into Welbourn's characterization of independent Churches in general as 'a place [in which] to feel at home'.

As the mission Churches have grown larger, they have tended to neglect this function of creating a home for their members. But the Holy Spirit Churches, even when their membership increases, keep the individual congregations small, so that the intimacy is retained. This is probably an important reason why many people prefer to join them rather than a mission Church.

Another, probably equally important, reason for the popularity of the Holy Spirit Churches is the theological content of their religious practices. Though they may not see the full significance of the person of Jesus as both God and man in one, which might explain why his death and resurrection are not in themselves regarded as sufficient for man's salvation, they nonetheless see his death as the event through which God made man's salvation possible. They are therefore truly Christian Churches. However, for this salvation to be effectuated, people must be purified through the confession of their sins before they can receive the Holy Spirit, which they regard as the real saviour for man today, for only its power is able to overcome Satan and all his evils. Although only the Holy Spirit can lead people to heaven, it is not seen as separate from God and Jesus. It is seen as part of the Trinity, that part which makes God and his power to defeat all kinds of evil present for human beings.

Their belief that the Holy Spirit brings God near to people and fights on their side against Satan is reinforced by their actual experience of it — it is not merely an object of faith — and this makes them feel keenly that it is indispensable for both their lives on earth and their eternal salvation in heaven. This real experience of God through the Holy Spirit, in and of itself makes the Holy Spirit Churches more attractive than the mission Churches, whose members are expected *only* to believe in, but not actually to see, God.

In addition, the Holy Spirit Churches have incorporated a number of traditional beliefs and practices into Christianity. For instance, the traditional 'hair-shaving' ceremony three days after a funeral is now interpreted as the resurrection; and the traditional sacrifice about three months after death to establish the status of the departed spirit in the spirit world has now been replaced with a ceremony 40 days after the funeral to celebrate the dead person's 'ascension', i.e. to establish the status of the departed soul in heaven. Similarly, ancestral spirits were traditionally thought to communicate with human beings in much the same way as the Holy Spirit is believed to speak to people through dreams, or prophets are thought to reveal people's hidden sins through the power of the Spirit. The battle between good and evil powers, between angels and the Holy Spirit on the one hand and Satan with his demons on the other, is also envisaged in much the same way as the fight between good and evil in the traditional Abaluyia religion.

These and other parallels with the traditional religion are by no means seen by members of the Holy Spirit Churches as a return from Christianity to the old religion. Followers of the traditional religion 'worship other gods', and this is a very serious sin in the Holy Spirit Churches. Rather, the members of the Holy Spirit Churches regard the incorporation of traditional elements into Christianity as a natural development. And because it is natural to them, it helps them reach a deeper understanding of their Christian faith. To use Sundkler's words, they regard their Churches as definitely Christian, but 'adapted to their own real needs' (Sundkler 1963). Through this adaptation, through interpreting Christianity in ways that are meaningful to their members, the Holy Spirit Churches have managed to integrate all their religious beliefs and practices into a whole, and have therefore created, at the spiritual level also, 'a place [in which] to feel at home'.

References

Anon. (1958) *Tsinyimbu Tsyo Kwidzominya Nyasaye*, East Africa Yearly Meeting of the Religious Society of Friends, Kisumu

Baëta, C. G. (ed.) (1968) *Christianity in Tropical Africa*, Oxford University Press, Oxford

Barrett, D. B. (1968) *Schism and Renewal in Africa: An Analysis of Six Thousand Contemporary Religious Movements*, Oxford University Press, Nairobi

Barrett, D. B., G. K. Mambo, J. McLaughlin and M. J. McVeigh (eds) (1973) *Kenya Churches Handbook: The Development of Kenyan Christianity, 1498–1973*, Evangel Publishing House, Kisumu

Beyerhaus, P. (1967) 'Kann es eine Zusammenarbeit zwischen den christlichen Kirchen und den prophetisch-messianischen Bewegungen Afrikas geben?', *Evangelisches Missions Magazin*, 111 (1), pp. 12–28 and 111 (2), pp. 78–87, Basel

Chilson, A. B. (1925) *Report of Native Affairs Committee, December 31, 1925*. Archives at the office of East Africa Yearly Meeting of Friends, Kaimosi

— (1927) *Personal Report of Arthur Chilson, 1927*. Archives at the office of East Africa Yearly Meeting of Friends, Kaimosi

Chilson, B. H. (1943) *Ambassador of the King*, Wichita, Kansas

Constitution (n.d.) *Constitution and Rules for the African Church of Holy Spirit*, African Church of Holy Spirit files, Lugala headquarters

Greschat, H.-J. (1969) 'Dini ya Roho', in H.-J. Greschat and H. Jungraithmayr (eds), *Wort und Religion: Kalima na Dini*, Evangelischer Missionsverlag, Stuttgart

Hollenweger, W. J. (1972) *The Pentecostals*, SCM Press, London

Hoyt, A. H. (1971) *We Were Pioneers*, Wichita, Kansas

Ingham, K. (1966) *A History of East Africa*, Longmans, Green, London (3rd edition)

Kay, S. (1973) 'The Southern Abaluyia, the Friends Africa Mission, and the Development of Education in Western Kenya, 1902–1965', unpublished Ph.D. thesis, University of Wisconsin

Kenya Government (1950) *Report of the Commission of Inquiry into the Affray at Kolloa, Baringo*, Government Printer, Nairobi

Keverenge, Bishop Eliakim, Javan Kasei and Manoah Lumwaji (n.d.) 'The History of the Lyahuka Church of East Africa', duplicated paper

Lonsdale, J. M. (1964) 'A Political History of Nyanza 1883–1945', unpublished Ph.D. thesis, Cambridge University

— (1970) 'Political Associations in Western Kenya", in R. I. Rotberg and A. A. Mazrui (eds) *Protest and Power in Black Africa*, Oxford University Press, New York

McVeigh, M. J. (1974) *God in Africa: Conceptions of God in African Traditional Religion and Christianity*, Claude Stark, Cape Cod, MA and Hartford, VT

Mahasi, Joseph (1974) Text of speech delivered to the participants of the advanced south leadership course at Limuru Conference Centre on 24 April 1974

Mavuru, Kefa Ayub and Peter Ihaji (1975) *African Church of Holy Spirit: Historia*, pamphlet distributed by the Church on 24 April

Mbiti, J. S. (1969) *African Religions and Philosophy*, Heinemann, London

Minutes, Friends Africa Mission. 18th October 1926, Archives at the office of East Africa Yearly Meeting of Friends, Kaimosi

Mpango wa Mazishi (n.d.) Typescript in the files of the African Church of Holy Spirit, Lugala headquarters

Muga, E. (1975) *African Response to Western Christian Religion*, East African Literature Bureau, Nairobi

Native Affairs Committee (1926) *Report of Native Affairs Committee: 1926*, Archives at the office of East Africa Yearly Meeting of Friends, Kaimosi

— (1932) *Report of Native Affairs Committee: 1932*, Archives at the office of East Africa Yearly Meeting of Friends, Kaimosi

Native Intelligence (1940) *Extract from Report by O/C Native Intelligence, 1940*, DC/NN.l0/1/3, Kenya National Archives

North Kavirondo District (1917) *Annual Report 1917*, DC/NN1/1, Kenya National Archives

- (1923) *Annual Report 1923*, DC/NN1/4, Kenya National Archives
- (1930) *Letter from DC North Kavirondo to PC Kisumu, 16th April 1930*, DC/NN/11, Kenya National Archives
- (1931) *Annual Report 1931*, DC/NN1/12, Kenya National Archives
- (1932) *Annual Report 1932*, DC/NN1/13, Kenya National Archives
- (1933) *Annual Report 1933*, DC/NN1/14, Kenya National Archives
- (1934) *Annual Report 1934*, DC/NN1/15, Kenya National Archives
- (1938a) *Annual Report 1938*, DC/NN1/20, Kenya National Archives
- (1938b) *Letter from DC North Kavirondo to PC Nyanza Province, 14 November 1938*, DC/NN.l0/1/1, Kenya National Archives
- (1939) *Letter by DC North Kavirondo 5 January 1939* DC/NN.10/1/1, Kenya National Archives
North Nyanza District (1952) *Annual Reports*, DC/NN.1/34, Kenya National Archives
Oliver, R. (1967) *The Missionary Factor in East Africa*, Longmans, London (2nd edition)
Painter, L. K. (1966) *The Hill of Vision*, The English Press, Nairobi
Peel, J. D. Y. (1968) *Aladura: A Religious Movement Among the Yoruba*, Oxford University Press, Oxford
Ranger, T. O. (1968) 'Connections between "Primary Resistance" Movements and Modern Mass Nationalism in East and Central Africa', *Journal of African History*, 9 (3 and 4)
Rosberg, C. G. and J. Nottingham (1966) *The Myth of Mau Mau: Nationalism in Kenya*, Frederick A. Praeger, New York
Salvation Army (1931) *Letter to Colonel Wilson, Commander, Salvation Army, Nairobi, 7th July 1931*. Archives at the office of the East Africa Yearly Meeting of Friends, Kaimosi
Sangree, W. J. (1966) *Age, Prayer and Politics in Tiriki, Kenya*, Oxford University Press, London
Sundkler, B. G. M. (1963) 'What is at Stake?', in V. E. W. Hayward (ed.) *African Independent Church Movements*, Edinburgh House Press, London

— (1970) *Bantu Prophets in South Africa*, Oxford University Press, London, (2nd edition)
Taylor, J. V. and D. A. Lehmann (1961) *Christians of the Copperbelt: The Growth of the Church in Northern Rhodesia*, SCM Press, London
Tempels, P (1969) *Bantu Philosophy*, Présence Africaine, Paris
Turner, H. W. (1967a) *History of an African Independent Church*, Vol. I. *The Church of the Lord (Aladura)*, Clarendon Press, Oxford
— (1967b) *History of an African Independent Church*, Vol. II. *The Life and Faith of the Church of the Lord (Aladura)*, Clarendon Press, Oxford
Wagner, G. (1949) *The Bantu of North Kavirondo*, Vol I. Oxford University Press, London
Welbourn, F. B. (1961) *East African Rebels*, SCM Press, London
— (1963) 'The Importance of Ghosts', in V. E. W. Hayward (ed.) *African Independent Church Movements*, Edinburgh House Press, London
— (1969) 'Spirit Initiation in Ankole and a Christian Spirit Movement in Western Kenya', in J. Beattie and J. Middleton (eds) *Spirit Mediumship and Society in Africa*, Routledge & Kegan Paul, London
Welbourn, F. B. and B. A. Ogot (1966) *A Place to Feel at Home: A Study of Two Independent Churches in Western Kenya*, Oxford University Press, London
Were, G. S. (1967) *A History of the Abaluyia of Western Kenya c.1500–1930*, East African Publishing House, Nairobi
— (1973) 'The Changing Concept and Role of Religion in Society: Interaction of African Religion with Christianity in Western Kenya', paper presented at the Department of History, University of Nairobi
Whisson, M. G. (1964) *Change and Challenge: A Study of the Social and Economic Changes Among the Kenya Luo*, The Christian Council of Kenya, Nairobi
Wipper, A. (1970) 'The Gusii Rebels', in R. Rotberg and A. Mazrui, *Protest and Power in Black Africa*, Oxford University Press, New York
— (1971) 'Elijah Masinde — a Folk Hero', in B. A. Ogot (ed.) *Hadith 3*, East African Publishing House, Nairobi

— (1974) *Towards a General Explanation of Protest Movements in Kenya*, University of Nairobi, Department of Sociology Seminar Series, Paper no. 2, August

Worsley, P. (1968) *The Trumpet Shall Sound: A Study of 'Cargo' Cults in Melanesia*, Macgibbon & Kee, London

List of Interviews

Amiani, Nathan — priest of the Lyahuka Church of East Africa, Chanda church, 12 April 1975

Eshera, Jotham — general secretary of the Lyahuka Church of East Africa, 8 March, 12 April, 13 April and 29 April 1975

Ihaji, Peter — secretary of the African Church of Holy Spirit, 25 June 1975 and 1 February 1976

Kadali, Enis — founder of the Gospel Holy Spirit of East Africa, 23 March and 30 June 1975

Kasei, Javan — treasurer of the Lyahuka Church of East Africa, 4 January 1975

Keverenge Atonya, Eliakim — Bishop of Lyahuka Church of East Africa, 28 December 1974, 2 January, 3 January and 27 June 1975

Keya, Nathan — secretary of the Gospel Holy Spirit of East Africa, 1 March and 7 March 1975

Lumwagi, Manoah — son of the Bishop of the Lyahuka Church of East Africa, 12 February, 17 February, 13 April, 23 June and 24 June 1975

Malao, Timona Luvai — quarterly meeting leader of the Gospel Holy Spirit of East Africa, 6 April 1975

Malolo, Zebedaioh — priest of the Gospel Holy Spirit of East Africa, 14 June 1975

Malongo, Thomas — priest of the Gospel Holy Spirit of East Africa, 7 March, 27 April, 9 May and 10 May 1975

Mandwa, Peter — leader of the Nairobi branch of the African Church of Holy Spirit, 25 December 1974

Mavuru, Kefa Ayub — High Priest of the African Church of Holy Spirit, 24 January and 10 June 1975, and 9 March 1976.

Murila, Jeremiah — provincial education officer, Western Province, a nephew of Kefa Ayub Mavuru, 26 June 1975

Ndagona, Musa — pastor in the Lyahuka Church of East Africa, 13 April 1975

Ondolo, Christopher — secretary of the Holy Spirit Church of East Africa, 27 January 1975

Sagida, Elfas Ojiango — chairman of Gospel Holy Spirit of East Africa, 1 March 1975

Shitsimi, Timotheo Hezekiah — general superintendent of the African Church of Holy Spirit, 20 February and 28 March 1975 and 3 June and 6 June 1976

Sida, Petro — village meeting leader of the Gospel Holy Spirit of East Africa, 22 March, 13 June and 14 June 1975

Wakhisi, Charles — associate secretary for missions commission, East Africa Yearly Meeting of Friends, 24 January and 24 June 1975

Zale Ambula, Japhet — Archbishop of Holy Spirit Church of East Africa, 19 December 1974, 13 January, 27 January, 2 May and 16 June 1975, and 15 March 1976

Index